55 Years Before the Mike

55 Years Before the Mike

by
Bob De Haven

TJ D

JAMES D. THUESON, PUBLISHER
Minneapolis

James D. Thueson, Publisher
Box 14474
Minneapolis, MN 55414

For Harriet

Thanks for your years of help and your inoperable kindness.

Foreword

Bob De Haven has been around at least as long as I have, which certainly entitles him to be called "the veteran . . ." You can see the problem there: I stopped when confronted with having to say "veteran WHAT." Because he is unclassifiable — veteran writer, certainly. And veteran broadcaster. And veteran Minnesotan, with some obscure ties to Wisconsin and elsewhere. Veteran tennis player, and raconteur, and charming self-promoter. Veteran Institution, I guess, with de facto Landmark status in the land of lakes.

And veteran befriender of people on the way up, and probably also of people on the way down. He had an unusual method of dealing with associates of less prominence: he listened to them and thought of them as people. I know; he made me feel like a People in days when I wasn't all that sure. He has a nice quality — you find yourself saying, even now, "If Bob De Haven likes me, I can't be all bad."

I remember the first time my wife and I went to his house. As we left he stood in the doorway and called, "*Now* who owes who!" Well, we all owe Bob, one way or another. Like so many things between himself and other people, he makes that debt a light and pleasant burden.

Harry Reasoner

New York City, March 20, 1985
(Roughly 35 years after first meeting Bob De Haven)

55 Years Before the Mike

Chapter One

It's colder than it really is.
— *on radio*

INDEED, it was colder than it really was when I reached the stairs leading to the WIBA studios over the Strand Theater on Capitol Square, Madison, Wisconsin, October, 1930, 2:30 A.M. Unlike Lord Byron the day following the appearance of *Childe Harold*, my nerves jangled a bouncy tune at thoughts of becoming a radio announcer at twenty dollars a week, a king's ransom that would establish me as a tycoon among the campus poor of that year.

The worn steps blurred under my long-legged leaps.

Little WIBA, owned by the Capital Times, and Bill Evjue, its famous liberal editor, elected to broadcast all night to alert its modest audience to the spectacle of the local station reshaping itself with new programs and new personalities of which I was one. Until now I never considered the dubious value at which the manager rated me when he slotted me at 3:15 a.m.

Our call to Madisonians was for them to repair their crystal receivers or buy new ones; don't miss the coming fun, stay up all night with our stars! 50 PEOPLE ON THE AIR, 50!! Orchestras, talk, singing — all night!!

In truth, backstage and backmike, we few who were promising such delights were in short supply of them and of the means of producing them for the air. Short of everything but exclamation marks.

Located on the theater's roof was a shed. A nice, tiny, 20th century-style shed, sided with corrugated steel. The WIBA studio, no plural. Two women waited for me, a red-haired pianist and a sixteen-year-old pop singer. The pianist worked in Cec Brodt's music store on State Street. Fifteen minutes of air time awaited them and me, the exclamation mark.

This studio, which also served as a business office, sported no sophisticated, scientific equipment, such as a signal light to indicate whether the mike was live or off and no gadgetry, such as a clock with a second hand to show the approximate time of night or day.

Upon my inspired guess that the magic moment of 3:15 had arrived, I stared out the shed window, across seventy feet of rooftop, to another shed which housed the engineering control room. The droopy eyes in the sunken cheeks of the engineer were looking for me. He was Reinhardt. Reinhardt managed a majestic wave of his hand, which I correctly interpreted as meaning, "Go ahead."

There I stood, a handsome six-foot Ferdinand Magellan, with an infant industry as cargo, courageous enough, even anxious to set sail on the unknown sea of broadcasting. And in this split second between the window and the microphone, I mumbled sage advice to myself, "You don't know how to do it; so your best bet is to be yourself."

That early morning I did follow my own admonition and coaching, and I have never changed policy from then to right now to this line on this printed page. At that mike I summoned my deep but natural voice, brightened by a congenial tone and manner, and split the air waves with a lightening strike of words of pristine originality, "Good morning, everybody, this is Bob De Haven."

Fifty years and a few more followed in which I earned a living, married my college sweetheart, who held down the wifely post with increasing intelligence and graciousness, raised four children on whom we showered Girl Scout cookies, orthodontia and college educations. I helped change the diapers, patch skinned elbows, attend class plays, while mastering the high wire walking that a (pardon the expression) public figure needs to survive and avoid jail. Our pay and fees were high for the times. Many of the volunteer jobs that went with the territory were time-consuming, even sticky, but always rewarding — recording for the blind, Church Warden, Minneapolis Board of Public Welfare, United Way Speakers Bureau, officering in a labor union, in two golf clubs and one tennis association. The towns were Madison, Wisconsin, Milwaukee, Chicago, Tulsa and the Twin Cities of Minnesota.

Girls and fellows are doing as well and better in broadcasting these days. They come from myriad small stations, trade schools and universities where "Communications" is taught (in my days communications was a telephone call not a school in a university). As a college sophomore, I enlisted in "Speech I" only to find the class was held in a building off my usual path — so I quit after one session — wonder what I would have learned in "Speech I"? Now, talent agents peddle this attractive broadcasting flesh, attending to their charges' looks on camera and their sounds when they make noise, directing their law suits. The performers in larger cities serve under contracts (contracts??) for six figures a year, easily covering the expense of costly hairdos, female and male. Women are important players in the game with their political clout that pushes them ahead in the hiring hall. All to the good I say. These performers, usually newscasters, earn in a year what a bountiful radio station in the Thirties would net in a year.

They mispronounce Hawaii, Boise and Vatican City, not forgetting Lima, Ohio, not spoken as is the capital of Peru; martial law becomes marital law; well, they sound alike, don't they? A Bishop appears on TV, attended by what the announcer calls crucifiers. Close to the proper word, crucifers, but no cigar. Some of the announcers' ad libs rise to the level of the expression, "You know ..." or, "I loved your book but I haven't had time to read it." One boob, interviewing a woman who had been held by kidnappers for two weeks, began with a brilliant question: "Will you ever forget being kidnapped?" The unfortunate lady should have answered: "I want to forget it, but I'll forever remember you — you asking this stupid question."

In the beginning, we were all poorly paid scramblers, striving to achieve steady employment. Agents to represent us, fight for us? "Ho, ho," to quote Santa Claus. WIBA paid me what I was worth, twenty dollars every Saturday about 4:30 p.m. Luckily I could read a written line and ad lib from here to signoff, if necessary, sometimes with brightness and humor. Good luck had directed me to study Latin in high school with Miss Foster and to study English as a college undergraduate and graduate. The Haresfoot Club, founded at Wisconsin around 1896, pitched me into comedy writing and acting.

Back there, we strove for acceptance in the free market of the mass audience, and engineering improvements helped immeasurably from crystal sets to tube to transistors. We fought as toy soldiers, challenging the newspapers, theaters and magazines. Hey, hear us — free! Had a kindly observer explained to us our brashness, we would have fled.

Now, too late to flee, I'll stand my ground and write my story, thinking that youngsters and oldsters will find pleasure in a light review of a time, light years away; a time called "The Old Days." My qualifications may be in dispute, except for one. I was there.

*   *   *

And along came Jack Carson (The following I wrote and broadcast on WCCO-Radio January 3, 1963.)

Yesterday the sad news came that Jack Carson had died. I've known him since 1931, when Dave Willock (currently playing the father on TV's "Little Margie") brought him to our room in the Royal Hotel, Milwaukee. Dave and I had an act, a comedy act, which he wanted to take into vaudeville, but I wanted to remain in radio and get married. Jack Carson was his substitute for me in the act, and the three of us that day and other days went through the act, rehearsing Carson in the dumpy surroundings of the Royal Hotel.

Jack was inexperienced but a natural-broad-shouldered, smiling, friendly, amused at things and people around him. He had no job — Depression, you know — so vaudeville was better than nothing. I remember one of the jokes in the act. Willock beautifully impersonated John D. Rockefeller teeing off at his golf course in Ormond Beach, Florida. Knobby-kneed, shaking and uncertain, cheeks sucked in, Willock would manage a back-swing of about ten inches, swing through, then shade his eyes to look far down the fairway. I, later Carson, picked up the ball a few feet away. (Laughter.) Willock pulled a coin from his pocket for a tip; Carson protested that the tip was only a nickel (remember, John D. was famous for giving away dimes). Willock announced quaveringly, "Young man, EVERYTHING is lower this year."

"Two Guys from Milwaukee" was a hot movie that starred Carson and Dennis Morgan. The two did not attend the University at Madison. Morgan graduated from Carroll College at Waukesha; for a short time, Carson attended Carleton College at Northfield, Minnesota. Carson told me that he developed a special dislike for one person at his college who had much to do with managing the daily chapel service. "A phony," were Jack's descriptive words. For revenge of real or imagined wrongs, Jack set a series of alarm clocks in the upper regions of the chapel so they would go off at intervals during the service. And they went off. And Jack was invited out. "Very clever," Jack commented.

The Willock-Carson act did tour vaudeville theaters and then broke up for reasons of starvation. Jack became the house master of ceremonies at the Tower Theater in Kansas City. The show changed weekly. Jack remained for two years. After one matinee in Kansas City, I went backstage to see him. The big fellow was unhappy about *his career, if he could call it that. He said, with hope in his voice, "I know a guy in New York who says he thinks he can get me a screen test. I'm gonna quit this place and go see him."*

Carson was a big success in the movies and went from run-of-the-mill parts at Warner Brothers to at least a pair of outstanding performances in "A Star Is Born" and "Cat On A Hot Tin Roof." He worked unceasingly — movies, nightclubs, radio, television. I did a turn with him for one of WCCO's Aquatennial shows. I remember one of the jokes. Jack said, "Bob, remember when we were kids in Milwaukee? Gosh, we had fun all summer long outdoors. Then came fall and Halloween. Remember that big house on Third Street with the little tiny house with the crescent cut out of the side at the back of the lot?" Bob: "Sure, I remember." Jack: "Remember at Halloween we used to sneak out and tip over — the big house?"

Once a friend spins to the top, the fellow left behind always wonders what his reception will be, and I was not optimistic — the worst maybe. Not from Carson. We were waiting for him at the Lakeside Golf Club in Burbank. Dennis Morgan, Bill Frawley and I. Jack arrived, bouncy and garrulous, the same old Jack. He told Bill Frawley that I had given him his first chance in showbusiness. That is true, if limited to merely quitting an act to make room for him.

Then, ten years ago, I suppose, we drove Jack and his wife, Lola Albright, to Northfield, Minnesota, to see the old school. The day was Sunday and the college President, Laurence Gould, met us all in his office. From there we went to the home of a pal of Jack's, Sid Freeman. Jack settled in the sunroom and talked. In half an hour Lola was urging him to his feet to keep a date with an old Wisconsin friend in Minneapolis. Jack rose to his feet, shrugged and said, "The story of my life. I'm happy here, and now somebody wants me to go somewhere else."

And the story of his death. He was happy here and yes-

Jack Carson, Bob De Haven, Stan Morner, Jr. and Dennis Morgan (Stan Morner) at Green Bay Packer football game in Los Angeles Coliseum.

terday Somebody wanted him to go somewhere else.
Hail and farewell!

Chapter Two

Jeanne Arland will sing 'The Nearness of You' after which
we'll play the Arrid commercial.

— *Bob De Haven*

MY EMPLOYMENT RECORD at the filling stations of the Gafill Oil
Company in my hometown of South Bend, Indiana, preserves
a commentary on the hard times inflicted by the financial
crash of October, 1929. (My college class was '29, and, in later
times, they called us "the last of the big spenders.")

In 1925 as a high school senior, I worked as an assistant at
everything at a Gaffill filling station for pay of 25¢ an hour.
While the calendars were turning to 1929, I earned a high
school diploma and then a B.A. degree and faltered into a jobless world. The Gafill people mercifully hired me again — at
30¢ an hour — showing the value they put on a higher education. As Ring Lardner wrote about a baseball pitcher who had
walked five batters in the fourth inning and walked only four
batters in the fifth inning, "This was an improvement, however slight."

No dawns broke in 1929 and '30; every day was dark. I have
never forgiven Chicago. We two brothers (Jim with his Wisconsin B.S. degree) would drive the eighty miles into Chicago,
lunch from a paper bag, spend the day looking for work, and
drive back to South Bend. At one newspaper building, I

entered the elevator, and the male operator of the lift asked if I was looking for a job. I nodded affirmatively. "Never mind going up," he advised solemnly, "You won't git a job." So I didn't go up; I walked disconsolately back to the street. Turned down, and I had not said a word.

Chicago was a mean, dirty, noisy, senseless symbol of failure. On the drive home, Gary, Michigan City and South Bend seemed slightly better because they weren't Chicago.

My children, when they have to, listen sympathetically to such tales. They hear but they can't feel. They listen, but they don't understand. And that's all right. Two of my kids even like Chicago.

Back at 725 North Scott Street, we boys were wanted and welcome. Pop had bought the place in 1912, brand new at $5,000 and made payments until his death thirty-two years later. As old Ted Lewis, the band leader from Zanesville, Ohio, recited, holding his clarinet, "I'm The Medicine Man For Your Blues." That was the theme of Pop and Mom. After the dismal and embarrassed reports of the wasted day in the big city, we responded to their magic nostrums of encouragement, music, laughter, never-ending kidding and the enduring grace of family love.

My mother, Daisy ("Hate that name," she declared repeatedly, "You call a cow 'Daisy'"), was a proud, industrious, intelligent, talented woman who, when in the mood, could brighten any room she entered. Part of her lot was discouragement, hard work and lack of fulfillment, but she could manufacture the priceless product of laughter. A visitor would start laughing when he came in the house, laugh while there and laugh as he departed down the steps to the sidewalk. Relatives, the trashman, mailman, milkman, neighbors.

A subaltern at the filling station ordered me to go to Mr. Gafill's home to shovel snow from his walks and driveway. My mother advised me to refuse and to quit the job. "You were hired to work in a station, not to be a handyman for old Gafill." I pondered her declaration of class war for sixty seconds, then left to shovel the snow; the job would take an hour's time and, at a rate of thirty cents, my attitude was strictly business.

— 19 —

Tipton, Indiana, was Mom's hometown, and there, in the Keleyla Opera House, she graduated with four others in the high school class of 1895. The Class Orator was Daisy Pauline (she hated Pauline more than she hated "Daisy") Whitinger. Her oration was entitled, "The Industrial Future of Women." Her daddy was a veteran of the Civil War whose pension helped send us to college. Daisy could play the piano and sing well enough to do the solos in the Episcopal Church choir. Pay — $1.50 per Sunday. One night in our Minneapolis home, she was darning socks while I was checking, on a record player, some items for an upcoming radio show. With no comment, I played "Ain't Misbehavin'" by Fats Waller. Daisy started to hum along and then said casually, "That's Fats Waller, isn't it? That's ragtime. Now that's the way we used to play the piano." On that same visit, I looked down our steep basement steps to see Daisy starting up, one hand free and the other circling her apron which held a pile of washed clothes. With hauteur, I called out, "Mother dear, all of these years you have worked for us children: now go out and work for yourself." Her laughter erupted to fill the basement and the stairwell; she leaned against the wall, let the pieces of laundry escape from her apron and sat down to laugh some more. That was Daisy's kind of joke.

Sundays were nickel-limit poker nights for the men, and, for all, homemade wine, good talk and a potluck supper (dinner was the noon meal, you remember). After the dishes were done, the ladies stopped the card game by filling the living room's chairs and davenport.

"Daisy, do Grandma." "Come on, Dais, Grandma!" These were demands that she create again her character of a creaky and crackly, ancient woman, intent on revealing tasty items she knew about and more that she was able to fabricate. Someone would toss a coat, sweater or shawl her way, and she would draw it over her shoulders, hunch forward in her rocker, move eyeglasses to the end of her noise, squint and lick her lips. Her laser gaze swept the room to flush out any imagined scandal. Her out-pouring was flavored with a ravenous taste for each item; she ad-libbed a stream of gags about the people present, moving, near to the end, to a dramatic level, hissing innuendos and breathing stealthy whispers when her news became sexy. My dad improved the scene by playing the part of the abused and maligned husband, shrieking protests that the old woman was nuts, that she didn't know what she was talking about.

"Now there's my two wonderful boys, James and Robert, sitting there as if they knew something, and John's boys, too — well (pause), he thinks they are his. Ain't those two handsome cherubs the very picture of their Maw and somebody else? Every Saturday night we corner 'em and bathe 'em because James acolytes on Sunday and carries the incense for the smell effect. Week or so ago, he dropped out of the procession and Rector Schottzenmeyer (how did he keep from bein' a Lutheran?), singin' away, kept singin' 'Where is the boy with the incense pot?' And little James, smart like his Maw, sang back, 'He dropped it in the aisle; it was too damned hot.' Now John, my husband, the repulsive one over there by the Victrola, seldom goes to worship because, he says, nothing ever happens except at weddings, which he does go to, and when they ask does anyone know why these two should not be fastened together, then John mumbles something in pig Latin that is only half heard and is really not a reason but does start the congregation to thinkin' and lookin' sideways and back and balls up Schottzenmeyer, which is awful easy to do or John couldn't do it."

Daisy would be on stage as Grandma for about twenty-five minutes. Daisy's was a class act.

My father grew up in Howard County, Indiana, where he was born in 1875. Soon his mother died. His father became sheriff (you can look it up in Kokomo, the county seat); as a ward of the only welfare system in place at the time, my father was shunted around the countryside to live with relatives, farm to farm, attending school and at last emerging from the eighth grade ready to work. Not harmed, not discouraged, but with a life supply of kindness and good will, he took on the world with a determination to escape from the bone labor of the farm.

John became a newspaperman and moved to South Bend in 1908 to take the reporter's job on The Times which had been vacated by Ring Lardner. "Lardner we poured on the New York Central, after a farewell party at the Oliver Hotel Bar, for Chicago where he had landed a job on the Inter Ocean, a newspaper." Lardner, who went on to become a humorist, sports writer and literary artist was ten years younger than John, born in '85, north, up the pike ten miles, in Niles, Michigan.

Christmas Eve, 1929 afforded an outlook as dismal as that of the rag-tag Galilleans looking for a night's lodging in Bethlehem. Kitty-corner from our filling station, the Men's Sunday School of the First Presbyterian Church had invited the people working on the four corners to cider and cookies. Two of us grease monkeys wiped our faces and hands, and, in sweaters and overalls, went across the street to the church. As William Wordsworth did write "my heart leaped up" when I saw my dad outside on the steps in the snow, shouting in his basso profundo, "Merrrrrry Chrrrrristmas! Come on in! Welcome! Everybody!" My pop in his natural role of party-maker and master of ceremonies.

He squashed social and ethnic barriers by not giving them a passing thought. Many years later, I was called into the manager's office of WCCO to meet a Mr. Brown from Fels Soap, Philadelphia. Mr. Brown asked me where I was from, then burst out with a tribute. "My God, I saw your name and guessed your father was John of the Elks Lodge in South Bend. Those Elks gave an annual Christmas party for poor kids. My name is really Brownstein, and I'm a Jew, and your dad came and got me one Christmas, took me to the Elks party, stayed with me and drove me home. What a guy! I ate everything in sight."

Pop never read H. L. Mencken that I know of, but he fulfilled that writer's epitaph: "If, after I depart this vale, you ever remember me and have thought to please my ghost, forgive some sinner and wink your eye at some homely girl." Pop was large in voice, humor and heart.

The big voice qualified him as a megaphone man, the man then as necessary to events attended by big numbers of people as the public address system and the bullhorn are now. Through his green-colored megaphone, four feet long, he could be heard and understood at the top of the grandstand or in the centerfield bleachers. With a two-sentence explanation, he once gave me his technique: "Don't jam the mouthpiece against your face; hold it off an inch or so. Don't holler. Let the horn do the work."

With Pop I learned about Jack Dempsey, George Gipp and the World Series of Baseball.

July 4, 1919, the autos raced at Springbrook Park, an amusement park near the city line between Mishawaka and South Bend, and Pop was on duty with his green megaphone. That was me, tagging along behind. During the racing program, he snapped at me, "Come on." Urgently we pushed through the crowd, walked out of the park and a few blocks east to the Half Way House, a saloon on the city limits. There he got some information from the bartender that seemed to please him very much and caused him to increase our pace to a dog trot.

To the racing crowd he spoke dramatically, "This afternoon, in Toledo, Ohio, in 100 degree weather, Jack Dempsey, the Manassa Mauler, became the new World's Heavyweight Boxing Champion by knocking out Jess Willard of Kansas. Willard's seconds threw in the towel before the fourth round started."

A mighty cheer from the grandstand met a cheer from those in the track infield. I shivered with excitement, still short of breath. The hungry challenger had knocked out the lumbering giant, the World's Champion. And my dad and I had brought the news from the Half Way House!

A newspaperman and somewhat of a public figure, my father was in on most things about town — sports, politics, rumors, facts. He was born, raised and always a stand pat Republican. In Indiana, U.S. Senator Jim Watson bossed politics during the Twenties; the solon remains dear to my heart for his reprimand to a freshman Senator, "Take it easy in your first years in the Senate. Like back home in Indiana. We don't care if the town prostitute comes to the Methodist

Church to worship, but she can't expect to direct the choir the first Sunday." My dad told me the Democrats never had run the country right. With such a reasonable stand, locked in such iron logic, following the G.O.P. was easy for me. When my first chance to vote for a President came in 1932, I was announcing at WTMJ, Milwaukee and introduced the presidential candidate, Norman Thomas on a feed to NBC. The white-haired, old Socialist spoke well and made sense. I listened carefully. I voted for him in a booth on the lawn of the Milwaukee Road Depot on Michigan Street. I should not have written home about my apostasy.

A crestfallen Pop wrote me about this wayward step, repudiating Hoover and Roosevelt. I wish I had his letter to type off for this book — you'd cry. Franklin D. perceived Thomas' political tenets and nostrums as I did. A few weeks after his election as President, he started to put into place the proposed Norman Thomas cures for the country's ills.

My dad was attentive to news and affairs at Notre Dame University, the wonderful school which was an easy hike along the St. Joe River from our house. He was a booster-sports fan on a first-name basis with some of the faculty, including K. K. Rockne, football coach. Knute and he were fellow Kiwanians. Annually, in September, Rock spoke to the luncheon club. Pop took me and Jim as guests. The famous character issued a stern dictum on the worth of football to South Bend. Stories and movies of his fight talks are not exaggerated. He shot his rapid-fire words that made fighters of every one listening. Fighters and believers. "Now Southern California is coming here to South Bend to play us. Here, not Chicago, as in the past, and this game will put us on the map, on the map, I tell yuh." Balefully, his small eyes covered the audience. At the end, that audience stood and cheered, and I actually left the hall with my fists clenched, ready for attack by any enemy of Notre Dame.

Rock and George Gipp were table talk at home. The Gipper had come down from Laurium, Northern Michigan, to play baseball at Notre Dame. Rock happened on some students kicking a football between two of the dormitories. One kicker made unusual height and yardage without seeming to try.

"Whatcher name?" the coach demanded.

"Gipp. I play baseball."

"Better try out for football."

Gipp tried out. (In one game he outran all defenders and sprinted toward the goal line, stopped, dropkicked the ball for the three points. He gave no reason.)

George Gipp was a wild one, endowed with superior skills and the erratic temperament that is dealt to geniuses. Essentially he did what he pleased and liked to do. Pool playing was a pastime; he easily picked up wayward bucks at Hully and Mike's Pool Room on Michigan Street from strangers in town who enjoyed inflated visions of their abilities with the cue. The locals who knew Gipp did well in their side bets. The young man became a football legend in his own time, shining as an offensive star on the field and cavorting on the campus and in town at night. He took sick, pneumonia, yet played in a game. I can hear now my mother saying, "People are on their knees on the sidewalks, praying for Gipp, in front of St. Joe's Hospital." Gipp died — a hero, the status he deserved.

Before the end, Pop and we boys motored to Cartier Field (pronounced "Car-tier," if you please, not "Car-tee-ay") on the campus to see Notre Dame play Purdue. Wooden bleachers, about fifteen rows high, lined one side of the field; fans stood on the other side on the ground and walked the sidelines to stay near the ball. We stood on this other side very near the scrimmage line. Gipp was easy for me to locate; everybody talked about him, pointed to him. Now, writing about this, I find I see well at this distance. Notre Dame had the ball on our side, near its own twenty yard line. The direct snap from center went to Gipp, and the cheers soared. Speed and grace made his movements thrilling to watch. Each of his moves was the right one. With the ball he lurched into right tackle, wriggled free of linemen, evaded the secondary down the middle and sprinted to the safety man; then this spot was usually filled by the defensive quarterback. Shooting to his right, Gipp eluded the last man and slowed slightly on his jaunt to the Purdue goal line. So I saw the great George Gipp play.

October brought an exquisite excitement to Main Street in my hometown. Over the sidewalk in front of the narrow building that housed the South Bend Tribune, workmen started to erect a one-story scaffolding on which would be mounted a twenty-four foot square replica of a baseball field. Painted green and white, the device sparkled in the autum sun, announcing that the coming struggle between the mighty National Leaguers and the upstart American Leaguers was soon to begin. Hundreds of baseball followers would fill the blocked-off street to watch the Series action reproduced on this wall. Our Ebbets Field, our Comiskey Park.

Ten men had parts to fill in operating this device. They met for pre-show discussions, rehearsals with imaginary plays and situations, for refinements in their coordination as team. The team lineups, weather and then the play-by-play arrived on a telegraph ticket in the fewest of words: "Base hit through shortstop. Runner stops at second," "Jones misses a curveball — his third strikeout." The team behind the board brought the game to life from the typed sheets hurried by office boys through the second floor window to the operators behind the ballfield board. And you can guess who handled the megaphone duties and who was at his side. (I was then training as a second-story man in anticipation of that WIBA studio in Madison.)

Names in the lineups were printed on cardboard strips that fitted into slots with moveable arrows to show the batter at the plate and runners on base. The white baseball was suspended by four wires attached to pulleys to send the wires backstage to a similar ball on a stick that an operator could move about the field.

Stand in the street to watch a ball game? A fake ball on a fake field? This was fun? You bet your New Departure Coaster Brake on your fancy bicycle! This was the World Series with every essential detail ... the entire ball game ... and you did not have to leave town to see it.

Pop poured the facts through his megaphone. "Killduff lobs a fly over the third baseman — it's a hit all right," and as he spoke, his Main Street fans saw the ball come down the lane to home plate, then shoot over third base territory. Slight pause for the left fielder to return the ball to the infield and then to the pitcher's box. "Killduff now on first."

Indeed, that number one bag was exactly where the real Killduff was standing on this day in 1920, this day that the gods of baseball had marked for an unforgettable event. Jim Bagby was pitching for Cleveland, Brooklyn batting. The World Series!

Next — Miller singled to fill-up first and second with no outs.

Next? Remember, you are standing on the bricks of Main Street over sixty years ago, and this is the World Series, not South Bend playing Peoria in the Three Eye League (Indiana, Iowa and Illinois, of course).

At a dead run the boy delivered the next yellow sheet from the ticket operator. Something big had happened; the boy tried to explain; he was too excited and could not. Four men and my dad went into a studied conference over the wire. The next play would be difficult to illustrate on the board and coordinate with the announcer. Not a chance to bungle. The manipulator of the ball rehearsed his moves in pantomime. Heads nodded to show their owners agreed and understood the procedure. As for my eyes and ears, they were popping.

"Ready, John?"

"Let's go," Pop answered.

John: "Mitchell is the Brooklyn Dodger batter. First ball over the plate is called a strike." Three more pitches moved the count to two and two, all appropriately produced by the ball's action on the board.

John: "Mitchell smacks a terrific, hard-liner to ... to Billy Wambsganss, second baseman. Billy holds the catch and (leaping excitement in the voice) steps on second base, fifteen feet from the catch, to double Killduff. Here comes Miller from first ... he's got to stop and run back ... (Pop is hollering now). Billy chases Miller and makes the tag! Billy did it — he tagged him out for the third out! A TRIPLE PLAY UNASSISTED!"

I'll add another holler, "IN THE WORLD SERIES!" The only such performance in World Series history, and you can look it up. If there was another, don't tell me. I was there in 1920. Ring Lardner wrote: "Billy Wambsganss, assisted by consonants only, today ....."

*   *   *

And along came Franklin Delano Roosevelt.

The man that day gave twelve minutes to important business in Milwaukee; he was campaigning to win his first election to the Presidency of the United States, making the year 1932. His train was enroute to Washington, D.C., after a final whistle-stop tour of the West.

Walter Damm, manager of WTMJ, and vice president of the Milwaukee Journal, was usually ahead of his competition, and he accomplished this by a rough-and-tough manner with everybody he dealt with. Naturally he was called "The Great God Damn." This fellow personally telephoned me and asked me to meet this particular train and talk into a particularly open microphone.

With one engineer, no producer, no director, no assistant, no other announcer, I went (oh, yes with one mike) to the Northwestern Railway Depot and set up on a baggage wagon where someone in overalls advised me the train's observation car would stop. That someone knew his campaign trains; the railroad engineer stopped his train so that the end of the last car was ten feet from my baggage wagon.

Already broadcasting, I stepped between the tracks and described what I could see inside the car. F.D.R. rose from a chair with the aid of two men and with obvious difficulty and pain. He couldn't walk; he shuffled, his oldest son on one side and a military man on the other. In this momentary and private view, the future President made a pitiable figure, unable to stand or walk alone, but plainly showing high courage in his ambition to win the leadership of a damaged and discouraged nation. Two chunky men who looked physically capable and humorless appeared to protest me and my position and my microphone, one of them commanding, "No broadcast ... No broadcast." Like the salesman who starts really to sell when

— 28 —

he hears the word, "No," I gave ground, retreated up the tracks, but continued to talk. These Secret Service men ignored me after I relinquished twenty feet of Northwestern tracks. Along with Roosevelt, the two must have been weary of the whistle-stop tour, or maybe I did not seem dangerous. The crowd of citizens pressed against a railing above and along a curve in the sidewalk which took the street's way along Lake Michigan.

These admirers were delirious to see the candidate when he appeared. They knew by his radio broadcasts. My position awarded a more subtle view. I was struck by the change in Roosevelt's manner and looks when he entered the open porch of the observation car and came into the crowd's view. F.D.R. was an actor going on stage. Weariness and pain were erased after a few blinks of his eyes; his concern rose from his steel-sheathed feet to the people who had come to greet him. He waved and smiled and saluted. Like Al Smith, he was a Happy Warrior. Then he started to speak and the crowd hushed. Briefly he commiserated with their economic woes, extended them the adrenelin of hope and made promises to be carried out if he were elected. Our mike easily picked up his speech for the radio audience. Cheers covered his farewell; the train started out of the station, and I signed off. A homely program compared to what the networks do now in presidential campaigns.

Back at the studio, I answered a call to the telephone. The Great God Damm was on the line: "That was a damn good broadcast!" Bang! He didn't wait for any comment.

Mr. Damm, I am inclined to agree.

*   *   *

Next year, we were married. That summer we parked in a space along the big lake Michigan, knowing F.D.R. was to speak to us and the country from his fireside. We were young, just starting out; we were not afraid, but we wanted someone to talk to us. Mr. Roosevelt did come through our car radio that night, and we felt better. I eased our tension by boasting,

"Why, Honey, that's the President of the United States, the guy I put on the air down at the depot. I taught him everything he knows."

Chapter Three

Nowadays a comedian gets an hour's experience then goes
on Johnny Carson's show.

—Phil Silvers

GOOD OLD KDKA PITTSBURGH. Radio sprang from its baby crib
around 1920 when KDKA broadcast the proceedings of the
presidential nominating conventions. When along came *I*, in
1930, the infant industry suffered growing pains, poorly diag-
nosed and faintly felt. The head phones (broadcasters today,
wearing their apparatus, look like the listeners of fifty years
ago) or horn-like speakers gave the correct time. Temperature
hadn't been yet invented. They gave you the next selection
that the string trio would play. Already you guessed that the
soprano soloist would sing "Ah, Sweet Mystery of Life." The
Coon-Sanders Band was belting "What A Girl" from Kansas
City with the singer of the two handling the lyrical excitement
... "What a girl ... what a night ... What a moon shining
bright." And this was in our own living room from "High
atop" some fancy hotel you never heard of until radio set up a
mike. Some programs of phonograph records enlivened the
schedule. Scanty news of the world and town was delivered at
unscheduled times, whenever the local paper was delivered to
the studio.

The receivers and their users were not choosy about the

people talking into microphones. Most any hard-up Merry Andrew of sufficient nerve or no nerves could qualify as a broadcaster. At first poets, students, drunks, hypnotists, college actors (me), elocutionists with diplomas, mind readers and tap dancers responded. We stood as a cross section of humanity, such a sampling as a prospective buyer receives when he plugs a watermelon.

My college buddy in the funny business was Dave Willock, a comic character on and off the stage. Dave must have given his Pa a chuckle in his mother's delivery. We teamed up in writing and performing in three Haresfoot Club musical shows. Each spring the club produced a musical comedy and a shows. Each spring the club produced a musical comedy and about sixteen performances on tour and in Madison. Our best towns were Milwaukee, Chicago and Madison. (Triangle at Princeton and Hasty Pudding at Harvard, Mask and Wig at Pennsylvania still carry on this way.) I had served a semester in Graduate School and was back on North Scott Street in South Bend about to hit Mr. Gafill for the third time for a job. Willock wired me: "THINK I HAVE US A RADIO AUDITION. COME QUICK." I came as quickly as the wooden spokes of my brother's 1922 Dodge car would carry me to Madison.

We auditioned something we had done for the Haresfoot Club's show promotion when, on tour, a station would give us time to advertise our show. We had christened our act with a name, "The Three Flying Filberts, Radio's Only Acrobatic Act." A third Filbert, the third nut, played piano as we indulged in ad libbed insanity/comedy in imitation of Sherman, Pratt and Rudolph, "The Three Doctors," a popular network act. To the tune of *A Little Kiss Each Morning*, we sang our theme, "Eight-forty-five each morning — eight-forty-five each night" to plug our times on the broadcast schedule. I can hear us singing now, I'm sorry to say. Willock and De Haven did get by, but sensational we were not. The following year, doing this same act, we landed on what we considered the big time, WTMJ, Milwaukee, where we got by, but a sensation we were not.

Within ten days of starting, I was given additional chores

Costumed for their Comedy sketch "All At Sea" in the 1931 Haresfoot Club Show (University of Wisconsin), Admiral De Haven and
Apprentice Seaman Dave Willock sit on a trunk at the stage door of
the Parkway Theater, Madison. Willock's feet, hands and face look
like those of a zany puppet. However, little Dave was for real and
very funny.

in Madison; the management made my twenty a week go a long way. At 5:15 in the afternoon, I came on the air as "Larry the Lamplighter," although there was electricity in the homes and streets of that decade, playing "Sweet and Low" as a theme on a reed organ and reciting poetry and wall mottoes about day being done. And, oh, I announced Big Ten basketball with Joe Steinauer, Wisconsin swimming coach, who then was famous for his advice given in an open mike during a recent football game, "Why don't somebody get that goddamned dog off the field?" I did a Madison Blues baseball game. Did I know how to do this kind of broadcasting? Well, no. From three to four in the afternoons I played pop records for the "Shut Ins' Hour." Saturdays, late at night, Willock and I did an hour from a roadhouse (now it would be called a night club) with Lanky Neal's Band, and I took my first drink of whiskey.

On a grim afternoon in late fall, the Capital Times desk telephoned that Knute Rockne of Notre Dame had been killed in a Kansas plane-crash. Sadly I announced that item on the air. If there is a Hall of Fame for radio announcers who have done a stroke-by-stroke broadcast of a chalk talk, save a place for me. The scene of my triumph was Madison's Lorraine Hotel. The cartoonist was Sydney Smith, creator of the Chicago Tribune's *Andy Gump* and *Gasoline Alley*. How I became mixed in this fiasco I don't remember. As broadcast material, a chalk talk rates with chess and a tatting contest for Ladies Over Eighty.

A casual visitor dropped in from Milwaukee where he was an architect and a part-time announcer on WISN. We talked. There was a job open at his station. I'm sure my ears turned red from excitement. I auditioned in the big town, got the job at forty dollars a week, and how many can increase their salary one hundred percent? On the first weekly payday at Mr. William Randolph Hearst's station at Michigan Street and the river, I carried the check across the street to the Gimbel's store cashier to exchange for four tens, then across a street again to the postal station in the Plankington Arcade to send five dollars to my Mother and twenty dollars to Theta Chi fraternity

— 34 —

in Madison for board and room already received.

Memorable during my short stay at WISN, remains an engineer named Johnny, a shrimpy, wild-haired blonde, and Post and Gatty. Johnny, my first day, boasted that he was famous for being able to start a record on the turn-table and on the air, dart into the restroom, take care of all his morning ablutions, except shaving, and return to the control room before the record played out, three minutes or less. Thus he accomplished a first in radio broadcasting, and you can look it up. In that year of 1931, Wiley Post and Harold Gatty flew around the world in eight days and fifteen hours in the *Winnie Mae*, named for the daughter of F.C. Hall, Post's employer. For older memories those names recall the delerium of adventurous flights of Nungesser and Coli (lost in the Atlantic), Lindbergh and Earhart. Milwaukee had planned a Post and Gatty welcome. Bells rang, sirens tore and guns exploded at the appointed morning hour. I grabbed a mike and a cord, climbed out a window to a roof (yes, another window, another roof) and greeted the silver ship as it came over downtown with pulsing words of welcome and American enthusiasm. WISN and I scored a resounding first. Well — for a short time it was scored as a first. We learned from the Milwaukee Sentinel newsroom downstairs that the flyers had come in to land at the South Milwaukee airport. The appearance over downtown was scheduled for later in the day. I had scooped even Post and Gatty. Four years later, Wiley Post and Will Rogers died in a plane crash at Point Barrow, Alaska.

At WISN I volunteered to do a broadcast, broad-recreation is more accurate, of a title prize fight being held in New York City, using the ticker tape report and injecting "life" into the strip of yellow paper with imagined action and details. This was commonly done in baseball then, and I aired many games that way, as did fellow announcer, Ronald Reagan, on WHO Des Moines.

The morning after this effort of the fight, the radio columnist of the Sentinel laid a scathing review on me, which, happily, I could not locate among the three pages of my life history. Somebody clipped the review and pinned it on the city room bulletin board. The mail brought me a rave review from a fight fan out there. Somebody pinned this letter to the bottom of the printed report. Then somebody (I'm tired of him) printed at the bottom of the letter in black pencil: "THE PUBLIC IS AL-WAYS RIGHT??" Distrust of critics still lurks in the caves of my mind.

During a night shift, I was idling in a WISM office, waiting to give a station identification at the end of the CBS feed of Guy Lombardo and His Royal Canadians. Kind reader, whether or not you are a radio announcer, speak those words aloud just for the thrill — "The music of Guy Lombardo and His Royal Canadians." Heady stuff, and I was twenty-two years old. The world was not too much with me, John Milton; the world was just right, the Guy was playing *Sweet and Lovely*, and the moon was on the river and I loved every bit of it and everything in it. Sweet and . . . . .

*   *   *

Along came Don MacNeill.

This tall, collegiate-looking announcer was already on the staff when I moved to WTMJ — hometown, Sheboygan, Wisconsin, and graduated from Marquette University. Don and I were the same kind of journeyman, writing our own stuff, ad libbing, being flip, funny or serious, but holding a show together. Genuine rapport with the audience and studio people came easily.

Saturdays the station moved an orchestra and cast to the Wisconsin Theater, the town's biggest, for an hour long show that was aired from the stage. MacNeill and I worked as a team. One night, for some reason in the script, Don was to pretend irritation in introducing an operatic number. In a hokey Italian accent, he thundered, "Vesta La Giuba — Pantsa La Giuba and Coatsa La Giuba. What's the difference?"

For the coming baseball season, I invented a character named Homer Benchbottom, a dumb rookie on the Milwaukee Brewer American Association baseball team. Don played Homer. A station salesman took us out to the Miller Brewing office to audition the act. Miller signed for the deal, calling for a show to precede each Brewer game. Low comedy, but topical, the dialogue was as fresh as the previous home game. After Don left, I played both parts, sixteen dollars a show for writing the script and acting two parts, the only parts. Wonder what Miller spends now for those TV sports commercials?

At 6 p.m. nightly, MacNeill did a successful turn with an orchestra and singers, which he called *The Dinner Club*. Success is no protection against dismissal, however. Before a year was out, Don and the management disagreed, and the big fellow packed his wife, Kay, and his vest, pants and coat for a retreat to Chicago to NBC where the moguls charitably gave him a week's tryout on a 7 a.m. dying show named, *The Good Morning Hour*.

Don changed the name and the week's tryout became two or three decades of work, which he renamed *The Breakfast Club*.

Three years afterward, I was "at liberty," a show business euphemism for the state of joblessness. At NBC in Chicago there was an opening as the star of *The Breakfast Club*. Don was leaving to do a nightly show sponsored by Tums and with a partner, Dr. Pratt of *The Three Doctors*. The nod came my way. Just like that. Next morning I spoke up as a network emcee, six mornings a week. I called my wife to come to town (with our baby girl).

Performing with the band and singers (Mary Jane Behlke and Clark Dennis) comprised my dish. I filled out the bill. Not so with another duty. Almost impossible was the switching of stations and groups on the console of buttons beside my mike. The emcee did the switching of the stations on the quarter-hour breaks? Ah, I kid you not. At "This is the National Broadcasting Company" cue, I punched out the network and punched in WMAQ, Chicago, on which I gave the call letters. (A lowly job for a star like I.) Then I hastily reset the network according to written instructions, showing the revised feeds, for the following segment. Are you lost? So was I. After that ridiculous button wrestling, I was supposed to come back and be entertaining. Well, I tried.

Don and Pratt were in less luck at 10:15 selling belly pills. The sponsor canceled, leaving Don unemployed for a day, after which he returned to the morning show, and De Haven was out on the street with his last pay check, his baby and his wife. What a business!

Chapter Four

My wife will buy anything marked 'Down.' Yesterday, she
came home with an escalator.

—Henny Youngman

AN OLD TIMER'S SCHEDULE on duty at the microphone could be
any hour, or multiple thereof, on any day. Once in our living
room, my wife and I reacted with surprise when a guest merely
observed, "Thursday is Thanksgiving." Holidays weren't
special; we celebrated them between broadcasts.

In and out of my scramblings over the years came people,
people, people. I did serve eight years as a Program Director in
Minneapolis. Any and every person with a mission concerning
anything outside of sales and engineering was sent to me, a
flood of humans, most of whom return now and in warm
remembrance.

One Sunday morning, my wife was waiting for me and sitting at my desk idly looking at letters prepared for me to sign.
One was addressed to Hope Titsworth. I had dictated, "Sorry,
we do not need a flautist." By now, I suppose, Miss Titsworth
is playing first flute or flaut in a heavenly ensemble, adding
some zing to the harps. My wife thought the letter showed the
rigors of being a radio station executive, and we privately
laughed. As such, people looking for work don't amuse; they
deserve affection and help.

An ordinary bloke showed up one morning, apparently to see what our little station (WTCN) was doing and to promote what he was doing. He explained his newspaper survey service, readership surveys, and that he was breaking into the radio surveying game and that his name was George Gallup. Cheerfully, since I was a willing audience, Mr. Gallup told me of a recent speaking appearance in which he described his method of gathering opinions. In the question period, a forceful lady demanded, "Mr. Gallup, who in the world do you interview for opinions and answers? I never heard of anybody who was questioned, and I know I have never answered any for a Gallup Poll."

He replied to her, "I'm not surprised, Madame. We can prove scientifically that only a small sampling of opinion will accurately give results that reflect the whole. You yourself have as much chance of being interviewed by a Gallup Poll-taker as you have of being struck by lightning."

Her protest did not end, for she said, "Mr. Gallup, I have been struck by lightening; now why have I never been interviewed by your people?"

Two well-groomed, well-painted young women arrived one early afternoon, one shy and uncertain, and the other an old friend, the former wife of a former announcer I had given a job. I thought they were looking for air work, and I carried on with my explanation of no jobs when I realized they were seeking business for a house of prostitution they had opened in a flat near the building.

Well before we entered War II, a skinny, black-haired young man sat down before my desk and immediately lit a cigarette. "I'm in radio news, just passing through and looking around. Going to visit my mother in Washington state." I believe if I had offered him a job, he would have unpacked his bags in my office. The fellow was Ed Murrow — "This . . . . . is London."

Clellan Card never did visit my office, but his image comes back. A long, pallid face, set in dead pan. He can only live on as a very special man and entertainer. Son of a dentist and of the Depression, he occupied the real world and also the world of his wacky comedy and off-balance remarks about the off-balance world. He gained early and enduring fame with the invention of a bird that landed on his window sill each morning. In his daily seven a.m. one-man show at WCCO, he recited poetry, delivered vocal essays, rattled sound effects and topped the fifteen minutes with a signoff, quoting the bird. "Birdie with the yellow bill hopped upon my windowsill, cocked his shiny eye and said, 'Hey, Miss Candy, let's go on a toot . . . . . sweet!' " Some of his act was done in a genuine Swedish accent, not the bogus vaudeville accent, he learned from an uncle.

I wish you all had been tuned in long ago when he broadcast his rearrangement of a sponsor's motto, "The Town Market Furniture Store, the Workingman's Furniture Store." This was a shlock outfit on Washington Avenue which was then Skid Row. The overlong, bombastic radio copy, for the announcers who read it on the air, was, at best, a stage wait that obstructed whatever else was going on. This time on the air, our Card read beautifully to the very end, then struck vengefully by chirrupping, "The Town Market Furniture Store, the Ferking Man's Wurniture Store."

This merry soul and his wife, Marion, raised a family of three boys, two of whom were killed within a six months period in airplane and auto accidents. They overcame the tragedies. Card fought their fate to defeat by spending the rest of his life entertaining children on a TV show called *Axel and His Tree House*.

One Saturday morning Elmer Burnham showed up at my office. Elmer was my high school coach in football (we tied Gary in the final game) and tennis; he was a fine product of the Springfield YMCA College. Old coach had moved to Purdue to join Noble Kizer's football staff, and, on Noble's death, Burnham took the top job. Purdue this Saturday was the University of Minnesota's opponent at Memorial Stadium. I was one of the four ready to air the game that afternoon on WTCN.

We shook hands vigorously ... Old coach with big teeth, sandy hair, build of an athlete and, as always, a friendly mien and open manner.

"But you've got a football game," I exclaimed.

"Not quite yet, and if you aren't ready by Saturday morning, you never will be ready."

He was ready because Purdue won (14-0, I think), and Elmer went on the air on our after-game broadcast.

Fifteen years later, Burnham had moved to Rochester University in New York state. My home phone rang and a Bill Hughes was on the line, asking quick questions to establish that I was the Minneapolis broadcaster and the one known to Elmer Burnham, formerly of South Bend. Indeed I was that one.

Hughes went on, "That Burnham is one wonderful guy. In Rochester, our backyards joined and Elmer was a second father to me, taught me basketball and football, never too busy to be a friend and pal. Well, when I grew up and got a job and was to move to Minneapolis, Elmer told me about you and the old days, and he made me promise I would telephone you and say 'Hello' for him ..."

My turn: "How long have you been living in Minneapolis?"

"Seven years," Hughes answered, losing no enthusiasm for Burnham and his promise to look me up. "And every time I hear you on the radio, I think to myself, 'Now I've got to call that guy up.'"

Sports talk brings in Dick Cullum, called by many, in addition to me, "The sportwriters' sportswriter." As a member of my small broadcasting crew for football, Cullum delivered expert opinion and useful background, without the corner-of-the-mouth smartness or silly Las Vegas savvy. We'd stop at the Tempo Bar after a football game and talk. In one of those booths, after one of those games, during World War II, Dick Cullum released an opinion I want to put into print.

Al Gowans, a football coach himself, spoke: "Well, fellas, we lost the game today, but I think the Minnesota players are having more fun. Bernie Bierman we lost to the U.S. Marines. Coaches don't coach alike; this Gopher team under George Hauser is having more fun, although not winning them all."

"I'm not sure I agree," Cullum interrupted, "Bernie was tough all right. He made them do four laps after scrimmage and gave them no drinking water until after practice, and he won't speak to any player on campus until that player had graduated. That's rough treatment — Bierman treatment. But a lot of guys went through that with Bernie, and they cussed him and threatened to quit, but they didn't. Then those guys in 1934 and '35 ended up National Champions. Now you tell me that isn't fun?"

Claude Radcliffe, "Rad," sat in my office many times. He and his wife were old time vaudevillians, songs and dances, funny costumes, two canes and a way with kids. They were poor as any around old WTCN, but Rosie and Rad trouped doggedly on personal appearances to play for kid audiences in a show that Rad, with heart trouble, closed with a clog dance. He'd finish with his red face and crooked nose beaming with pleasure. On the air he did a kid show at 7:20 a.m., only five minutes long. I'm sure his fee was small, and I'm pleased I can't remember the figure. And some readers might smile indulgently at the motto saying the show must go on. Well, don't. One morning at 4:30, my bedside phone rang, "This is Rosie. Rad won't be there this morning. He died last night."

Those kinds of people to the end, and the past the end, take care of their professional engagements.

Most office callers were looking for work; my job was to turn them all down. This I did do, not hasitly or preemptorily or without advice and some encouragement. They marched in — writers, actors, musicians., announcers and some individuals with no vague idea of where they might fit into a radio station. They were all interviewed with courtesy and understanding; Lord knew I understood; my salary was $225 a month and one job from the street myself.

Arthur Naftalin reached our receptionist (her title was "Telephone Girl") one day when I was anxious to vacate my digs to take lunch and a swim at the YMCA. Mr. Naftalin, dark-haired, serious, about thirty, entered with two gentlemen friends in tow. One was named Ed O'Brien, and the other, for the moment, let's call The Third Man. They were buddies studying and teaching in the Political Science Department of the University of Minnesota and not among the run-of-mine callers on this little Program Director. Theirs was a drive for effective places in local and state politics, and their idealistic vision revealed a possible better world. With honesty and candor, they proposed an interesting plan for The Third Man.

"Our friend here wants to run for office, for mayor of Minneapolis to start with, but nobody knows him. He's dedicated and smart; he is a terrific speech maker, makes friends quickly and impresses them — good memory, impeccable ideals and plenty of energy. He could pull a fire wagon." The lecture raced on, Naftalin talking; the other two nodding. "Obviously, the quickest and best way to become widely known to the general public is to go on the radio. We want to put our friend here on the air on your station so he can become a candidate with a running start."

Hubert Horatio Humphrey, son of a South Dakota pharmacist, sat smiling his approval and appearing to be every inch the remarkable man Mr. Naftalin was describing.

After a half hour's good talk among the four of us, I declared the idea appealed to me and that I would consider the offer, along with the scheduling and fee. A week later, a deal resulted.

Hubert went on the air with a fifteen minute news and news commentary program, four nights a week at 9:15, for twenty dollars a week. Oh well, I had given a job to the future Vice President of the United States; another day at the office.

A radio sensation Hubert was not; his voice was high and stringy; his reading skill was there but occasionally faltered; as was to be expected, he sounded like a beginner. Plusses were: his confidence in handling news subjects and the quality of his background and commenting on larger events in the news. Hubert's political loyalty and personal convictions (he was a Democrat and yet to found the Democratic-Farmer-Labor party in Minnesota) properly caused no bias in his presentation. Hubert and I became close friends in our informal hired hand-boss relationship.

The hard noses in the sales department sniffed no big money for the station in the new deal; some efforts were made to land a sponsor with no luck. There was no perceived improvement through Hubert in our news service for our audience or in upping our station's acceptance. In the stated purpose of the Political Science pals, Hubert's air work was less disappointing. Hubert was ripe for takeoff into Minnesota's politics, and he was the most well-equipped and eager discovery in the history of the game. Hubert was needed. Immediately he became the hottest weapon in his party's arsenal; he took off sensationally and soared like a rocket that only his death brought to earth.

At WTCN, he missed one or two broadcasts, never without adequate notice to me, however; then his misses increased to one or two per week. Each time he ran into scheduling problems with his speech-making for the Party. I was faced with letting him go, always my most difficult duty. I postponed action for a week and then telephoned him. Typically, Hubert beat me to my point.

"Bobby, I'm sorely afraid this arrangement is not going to work, much as I love to broadcast, but I can't do it justice and take care of the demands for me to speak. Politics is really my choice, as you know. It isn't fair for me to tie you up with that air schedule and me not to hit the ball for you every night. Not possible."

Hubert said more, of course, but that essentially was his conversation. Both of us were off the hook.

How to win friends and influence people? Hubert could have written that book.

He was defeated in his first run for public office, that of Mayor of Minneapolis, and then, two years later, defeated Marvin Kline for Mayor, the man who had defeated him in their first contest. He then rode into the United States Senate with a stunning victory at the polls over Joe Ball, a Saint Paul newspaper reporter who had been appointed to the high office. The peppery druggist, who wanted to become known, qualified for a place in the hearts of Americans. He became Vice President, unsuccessful in a run for President, a smashing victor, again, in trying for the Senate. His grave is across Lake Calhoun from where I live now in Minneapolis, a mile away.

His wonderful wife, Muriel, helped in his struggles in

world and national affairs. She and I used to sit side-by-side at the Mayor's Luncheon annually, a part of the Aquatennial, a Minneapolis summer festival. She was the mayor's guest of honor; I was master of ceremonies. During one of the luncheons, I remarked to Muriel that I had been on the same job at three affairs in the past.

She answered, "I've attended all of them. This is my sixteenth."

Hubert and I sat together at an affair in January, 1976, arranged by the Minnesota Press Club. Hubert appeared as the honored object of a political roast, and I performed as master of ceremonies.

Several of the speakers made fun of Hubert's penchant for speaking at great length and often. I devised a tale of his broadcasting days, of a time when the news machine fouled and there was no copy. Hubert was undismayed. He promised, "Put the mike and the clock in front of me, and I'll fill the time."

Muriel at this event spoke briefly and amusingly.

"Hubert was always a good talker, even way back in South Dakota days, and I suppose he fell in love with me because I became an adoring listener. I remember clearly the events of the night he proposed marriage. We were in his father's car, and he started excitedly in a rush of speaking and oratory. This went on. Three times I said, 'Yes,' before he stopped talking."

Arthur Naftalin did well as Mayor of Minneapolis, as an educator and now as a staff member in the Hubert Humphrey Institute of Public Affairs, a part of the University of Minnesota.

Muriel was appointed to the U.S. Senate.

*   *   *

And along came George Higgins, sports announcer.

He flourished in the Thirties among the Saint Paul sports people — baseball, football, basketball, boxing with Mike O'Dowd and Tommy Gibbons, who went the distance with Jack Dempsey at Shelby, Montana. His buzz saw voice and involvement with sports and its society earned him an audience for the small WTCN.

One night, he was announcing at the same pace as the two fighters in the ring, full speed, full blast. At home, listening, Higgins came through to me: "Kater lands two left jabs on Jones who slams back with a body right. They clinch! Kater attacks, Jones is wobbly but tries a looping right to the head. Kater lands, Jones lands. They're wild up there — Kater — WOW — Kater knocks Jones right on his . . . . . Jones is in a sitting position."

Chapter Five

You people don't realize that tourism is the backbone of
your bread and butter.
—*Representative Lloyd Kincaid (D), Crandon, Wisconsin.*

NOVEMBER 29, 1981, the toll call came in the early evening. I scrib-
bled notes with a pencil.

"This is Lillian of Dassel. How you been, Bob? Oh, I'm all
right — I live alone, but I don't get lonesome. I get breakfast for
a well-to-do woman, and sometimes she comes in here for
dinner. I used to be sort-of a nurse. I know a lot of nurses and I
can do what they did. My kid brother died a year ago. Six in our
family. I'm the only girl and only three of us left. I'm having a
beer right now — work and then have a few. Oh, I went to
Church. I did my good deeds for the day and now I'm relaxing.
No harm in that. Well, say hello to your wife. Good luck, Bob."

Lillian will call again; she has called at odd moments over
the past twenty years. Although I have appeared in her town of
Dassel, I don't remember meeting Lillian. We became friends
by her following me on the radio. No small thing in my life. I'd
rather have Lillian and the thousands of anonymous Lillians
than an undressed centerfold object whose name is on everyone's lips and loins are in everyone's barracks.

In the supermarket we frequent, a stranger, a little lady
whose chin reached about two feet above her pushcart handle

bar, blocked my passage and twisted her head so she could look up into my face.

"You're Bob De Haven, aren't you?"

"Yep."

"How are you feeling, Bob?"

"Okay, right in the pink."

"Have you got enough money to get along on?"

"Yes, I think I have."

End of conversation. She pushed on past the dry cereals.

She inquired for vital information. Was I in health and did I have enough money? She had certified our bond of friendship.

Years before audiences at fairs, streetcorners, schools, radio, television, colleges, farmers, unions, churches — those years paid me in coin dearer than that of the realm, in a genuine, comfortable feeling for people of the land, town and street.

In a Saint Paul children's hospital one morning, I did a radio broadcast for some of the patients. In the warmup before air time, I explained that we wanted a loud response, when on the air, to my opening line of, "Hello, everyone." The answer from the kids was to be, "Hello, Bob." As always in a warmup, the first attempt of the audience was tentative and feeble.

"Hey now," I said, "If you don't make more noise than that, people will think you have no pep here at Gillette Hospital. They might even think you are discouraged and don't care about being on WCCO this morning. Let's try it again. Same words but more noise and enthusiasm."

The second, "Hello, Bob," bombarded the walls of the room. The kids laughed and clapped at our success in raising their volume and excitement. The patient nearest me was a pale-faced boy, about eight years old, in a wheelchair, his legs twisted, his arms hanging. His head veered slightly from the natural posture, but his eyes were sparking with life and exuberant pleasure. His high voice slurred through his teeth and topped the other noises — "Wasn't that a wonderful 'Hello, Bob'?"

You bet that was, little fella. So wonderful that I'll never forget you and your shout and your love of life.

For about ten years, the same station sent me out weekly to

smaller towns to do shows in the stores of the Our Own Hardware chain. We were always greeted by townspeople and farmers who wanted to visit a live broadcast. (People still want to.) I was billed as "Our Own Bob" after the name of the store group. With the help of a musical group, I carried on from a stage usually constructed of packing boxes. Politicians, town characters and celebrities were introduced and interviewed, and, of course, the store owner. One Saturday in Woodville, Wisconsin, we drew more than the population of the town, right into the store. Our visits over the years dotted the maps of Minnesota, South Dakota, Iowa and Wisconsin.

Nothing in show business carries the impact of a personal appearance. The person makes himself special when he goes where you are and does his act and shakes your hand.

This letter came only yesterday, only twenty-seven years ago.

Wilson, Wisconsin

Dear Bob — Your "As You Like It" program has just been completed and, as far as I'm concerned, it's the best you have ever put on.

Your transcription from Theodore Wirth Park was really fun! Such things we common people like and we parents thrill to, even to the giggling, screaming birthday party. I couldn't help but think that your patience with the 'little sillies' must be a result of the stages your own daughters passed through. I guess you'll always hold a soft spot in my heart for memories connected with my own daughters. We were living at Luck, Wisconsin, at the time you put on a Saturday morning program at the Hallquist Hardware there. My girls, Faith and Phoebe, attended and were so thrilled. After the show they went to the drugstore and you were there. You talked to them and treated them each to a candy bar. They came home so starry-eyed and happy to think you paid attention to them.

A little over a year later our Faithie at 13 was struck with a bone cancer (a Ewings tumor) and after a severe

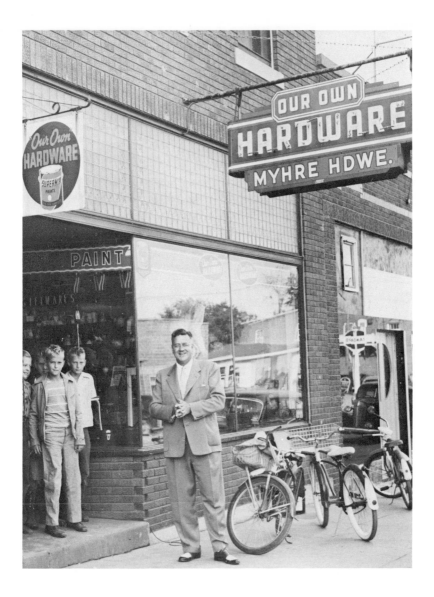

There's no Main street like the Main street of your hometown. Bob De Haven crisscrossed Minnesota and many parts of the adjoining states appearing on Main streets and in the stores of the Our Own Hardware chain. Here he is ahead of the crowd at 7:00 A.M. in Spring Grove, Minnesota (pop. 1,275) to do the "Our Own Bob" show inside at 8:45.

trial went home to be with our Lord. Happy as we know
she is, we still get lonely for her and are looking forward to
the day we will join her in glory.

At the lonely times, it is good to think back on the
things that made her most happy here on earth. So, do you
see why I, who mean nothing to you, have a special, kindly
memory of you? I've thought of this so many times, and,
after your program tonight, I had to write and tell you of
it.

> *Sincerely,*
> *Mrs. Stephen Sonmor*

Back in the Thirties, I was satisfied at WISN with my forty
dollars per week. One noon I stopped at the top station, WTMJ,
to meet a friend, and Russ Winnie, the honcho there, accosted
me.

"Why are you working over there instead of over here?" he
demanded. Making demands was typical of Winnie.

"Because no one asked me to come over here."

In a few days the deal was made. For three years I solved
WTMJ's problems, which glories will be recorded somewhere
on these pages. I'm moving to my next job jump, the one to
Minneapolis, which was achieved through a simple, vengeful
act.

In the WTMJ office, my desk was one of four in the general
office, but not the one nearest the door. That was occupied by a
nice enough filly named Sylvia who was all right until a
stranger appeared, and then she became overwhelmed by her
importance in show business. She was less than polite to
visitors with hats in hands, seeming about to ask for a job.

On this day, she was busy in another part of the building
when there appeared a small man of pale complexion with an
inch-long cut on his forehead which had been bleeding. Indeed,
he held his brown hat in his left hand. I bolted to intercept him,
saying to myself, "This is one guy Sylvia is not going to put
down."

The little guy was from Saint Paul, and we started to talk.

At dinner he related how he had cut his head in a sleeper car, and what was more important, that he was looking for a program director to come to his new operation, WTCN, in the Twin Cities of Minnesota. Here I was an annoucer; there I could be an executive. Onward and upward; you're married now with a child and wife. Life is real. In a few weeks, we left town in our 1933 Chevrolet, 4-door, radio, brand new sedan, $660.

1934. That has no ring to it. In Minneapolis, just before I arrived in August, truckers union members and other citizens had been killing each other in the famous strike that brought out the militia and made a national figure of Governor Floyd B. Olson. The cost of everything was rock bottom and no money to buy, even at rock bottom.

WTCN was owned jointly by the St. Paul Dispatch-Pioneer Press and the Minneapolis Tribune (W-Twin-Cities-Newspaper, get it?), the latter a reluctant partner. The St. Paul publisher, Leo Owen, pursuaded a relative, one of the Minneapolis owners, a Murphy, into the partnership. They bought a wheezing coffee can of a station called WRHM for $50,000; $25 million today might obtain you an interview to discuss the rest of the money for purchase of the properties. Comparing station deals of the Thirties to modern times seems the stuff of fiction. WCCO, phenomenal money-maker for sixty years, was first granted to Washburn Crosby Co. (WCCO, get it?) Henry Bellows, a milling executive and former member of the Federal Radio Commission, had landed the company's station on a clear channel, 810 kilocycles then I believe, a super position. One version with some currancy had Bellows at this point convince Stanley Hubbard of KSTP that the 1150 spot on the dial was more effective because it was a larger number. The opposite in the numbers game was true. Now the elder Hubbard seems too smart to fall for that come-on. At a luncheon, Donald D. Davis, then Chairman of the General Mills Board, told me the old company, Washburn Crosby, had tried to give the station to the City of Minneapolis. The Council demurred, and the offer was sweetened by a promise to pay any losses after the first year. A flat turn down.

A similar offer was then made to Saint Paul, which was answered by a flat turn down. Oh men of no vision, or beware of millers bearing gifts.

Our ragtag, WTCN crew had good people, used to the uses of adversity, convinced that a smile wins. They were underpaid; three engineers occupied apartments that were part of a trade deal for advertising on the station; one announcer, who was fully capable in his job, was paid fifteen dollars a week. Our broadcast signal was slightly stronger than the chirp of a baby chick; our offices and two studios were rent-free in the Wesley Temple Building in exchange for time on the air for the owner, Wesley Methodist Church.

Oh, yes, we could not claim all the air time; we shared with the University of Minnesota station, WLB; we had no reputation, except for not paying our bills, but we went to work to make people like us. We covered the State Fair with torrents of enthusiasm and some skill; we did University football and basketball; pro hockey (first in town); six-day bike racing, believe it or not; wrestling; boxing and whatever I left out. Holding our carbon mikes, we dove into waters that other stations had not discovered.

Here's an illustration of how we created a program where none was before. Returning from a football broadcast one Saturday, our sports announcer, George Higgins, casually said to me, "We ought to go on the air and telephone servicemen and let their families talk to them." I did the rest.

We named the program *Hello, Soldier — Hello, Sailor*; the time was Sunday afternoon, and it was sold before the first broadcast. Airing the incoming voice on a telephone was against the regulations of the times. We gathered parents, relatives and sweethearts in the studio. The prearranged calls were made through our switchboard to spots around the country. As master of ceremonies, I indicated the talk and reaction of the servicemen, and the radio audience heard the family members directly. Yes, it worked. The heart tugs, laughter, tears of a wartime family all registered dramatically and in proper taste.

An unexpected event of one Sunday put our crew to the test

In the WTCN show called "The Ladies' Friend" Bob fought 'em off for the camera. 1939.

of concentration and discipline. Just before air time of this particular show and during the warmup, our operator called in to tell me that the station's Musical Director, Frank Zdarsky, had suffered a seizure in his office that adjoined the studio. I found Frank sitting on a sofa, holding his head. "I'll be okay — I'm okay," he protested.

Five minutes to air time, I was interrupted again by the telephone. Our operator said in a quavering voice, "Frank is dead." We proceeded with the program.

Mike Coscio, an organist and friend of Frank's played "There's a Long, Long Trail" in the middle of the show, as I read a letter from a serviceman. Not a spectacular element of the show, but one that tugged the emotions of war. I could see that Mike was crying as he played, ducking his head toward the keyboard. His friend was dead. "Long Long Trail ..."

The telephone calls and the conversations went along perfectly. Off the air, I stood in front of the desk with the phone and microphone and said to the studio audience, "I suppose you are aware that a terrible event was going on backstage during this program." There was no response, no indication they had noticed our struggle. So I explained the death in the next office.

We didn't act like heroes; we didn't feel like heroes. We were not heroes, merely little people producing an inconsequential radio program in a tight spot, and the show did go on because we were little other things also — professionals.

*   *   *

Along came Lee Whiting and Russ Winnie.

Lee came along from the Minneapolis Journal to WTCN, a typical salesman, and that is meant to be a compliment; I like salesman. Energetic, optimistic, friendly, industrious. My only regret about this motto is that I did not originate it. "In business, nothing happens until someone sells something."

Lee and I ran WTCN during a year when we had no general manager. He was easy to fight with and easy to love.

In his newspaper days, Lee sold display advertising. One of his good accounts was Hove's Grocery, founded by the amiable, pious, God-fearing Peter Hove. The little man in his shined shoes, brown suit and white shirt, loved to stand near the cash registers, make his finger tips into a steeple, rock slightly back and forth, greet customers and listen to the tinkle of the money.

One Wednesday, Lee relates, he called on Peter to pick up advertising copy for the Sunday newspaper. Peter had not yet decided what to feature in his Sunday paper space.

"Mr. Whiting, I know you want this copy, and it is right that you should. I know the deadline is tomorrow, and I want to have that copy ready in time so that you will not be troubled by any inconvenience or tardiness. Mr. Whiting, I'll tell you what I am going to do. After the store closes at six o'clock, I'm going home to have dinner with Mrs. Hove. After dinner, I will move into my dark bedroom, sit down and think and pray, and the good Lord is going to tell me what to advertise on Sunday..."

At this point, Lee Whiting cut in crisply, "Peter, I don't care who is going to write the copy for Sunday, but I know I have to have it in the Journal office by three o'clock tomorrow afternoon."

Russ Winnie came along a few pages back, but you didn't meet him properly. Russ, just out of college, caught on with the Milwaukee Journal station, WTMJ. When I arrived there, in 1931, Russ was assistant manager, chief announcer, program director and sports announcer. This talented Winnie performed his executive duties and also announced all the Brewer baseball games, home and away. The away games came by ticker tape, and Russ put life into the bland facts that were telegraphed. Also, he broadcast the entire football schedules of the University of Wisconsin and the Green Bay Packers. That meant hard travel and hard labor at a difficult broadcasting art in which he was a pioneer. Saturdays he could be anywhere in the Big Ten for a Wisconsin game, Sundays in Green Bay or anywhere else in the National Football League (no air travel) and Mondays back to run the radio station.

At his side, acting as his football spotter and only assistant, sat his wife, Evie, whom he called "George" because women historically were banned from the press boxes. With this pseudonym and special permission, George played her most important part in bringing fame to WTMJ for faithfully delivering football. Walter Damm, Mr. Big at the station, gave the broadcasters his full support, fighting the NBC network for the afternoon time so imperiously demanded by the network for its own programs. I recall hearing Damm shout to Winnie, "If NBC doesn't like us taking Sunday time for the Packers, NBC can go straight to hell." Not polite, but decisive;

and, what's more, concerning local listerner interests and loyalties, Damm was damn well right.

Football is difficult to do on the air; Winnie invented how to do it. The talented and trained seals of today have had skilled help in growing into their jobs. Winnie sensed how to relay the action to the mike, the color and the flow of the game, to keep track of the ever-present twenty-two players, four officials (now, I think, there are eight) with occasional comments on the weather, cheerleaders, other game scores...Winnie could do it all. Evie, who survives Russ, annually awards a cup to a worthy Senior football player at Wisconsin.

In the recreation room of her home, there are, on the wall in a frame, comments of three radio fans on the ability of Russ Winnie.

Excerpts:

From "Roses and Thorns", a Milwaukee Journal column about radio:

"After hearing the Marquette-Wisconsin game, I must say that the great Russ Winnie gave an exhibition of one-sidedness that will never be matched. If Wisconsin made two yards, it was described as 'tearing, crashing, plunging' for the yardage. But, when Marquette carried the ball, 'Marquette advances the ball five yards'.

From Hans Ruedenbusch, Mayville, Wisconsin. (This fellow was tricky; he wrote the sponsor.)

Wadhams Oil Co.
Milwaukee, Wisconsin.
All afternoon Russ Winnie showed his true colors. 'The Marquette fans are thrilled at the prospect of a scoreless tie,' and 'Marquette valiantly stopped all of Wisconsin's running attacks.' It seems a shame that this very fine broadcast service should be handled by a man so anti-Wisconsin."

From the Johnson family, Chicago, Illinois.

"Hurrah for Russ Winnie! We liked the non partisan way he handled the entire broadcast of the Marquette game with the Badgers. To our way of thinking, there are only two broadcasters who know how to handle football — Ted Husing of CBS and you, Russ Winnie."

There you are. One game, three letters with three different complaints against the one announcer. The fellow is anti-Marquette, anti-Wisconsin and nonpartisan. I think of Abe Martin, the savant of Brown County, Indiana, who said, "I'm going over to the Poor House Sunday to visit a friend of mine who published a newspaper that would please everybody."

Chapter Six

In the ring, if I can find that man, I can hit him; on the golf
course, that ball defy you to hit him.
   —*Joe Louis in an interview at a golf tournament.*

THE MEMORIES OF EIGHT CHARACTERS (in search of an author?)
clamor to enter this history: Nat "King" Cole, an anonymous
sports announcer, an anonymous office secretary, Merle
Jones, Jimmy Cagney, John Cowles, Sr., Dick Enroth, Halsey
Hall and Paul Aurandt. With two other disc jockeys I was
called, as the saying goes, by CBS to New York to appear on
one of the summer replacements for the Chesterfield program,
featuring Ray Block's orchestra and guests. King Cole was the
guest when I appeared on the program. He ambled into the
studio-theater to a greeting from the regulars already on stage.
Smiling, handsome, lean and affable, Cole rehearsed quickly
with the orchestra and his trio. He came down to the seats to
shake hands with us from the sticks. Easy to see why
everybody liked Cole, a pianist who exceeded that talent by his
singing. Cole was black and he had class.

Ten years later, he was appearing in the South, doing
concerts. In one town, four men from the unruly audience
stormed onto the stage intending to attack Cole. Stagehands
prevented the assault; Cole escaped unhurt.

Inevitably he was interviewed by the press and asked how

he felt about the incident. Cole said, "I have nothing to say. I'm an entertainer, not a politician."

After I left KVOO, Tulsa, in 1938, a fellow came on the staff as sports announcer, the job I vacated. People told me he would not leave that studio during the dinner hour, when he had a break in his schedule. His explanation: "Suppose Babe Ruth died and I was out to lunch?" Babe Ruth did die, and I hope this eager kid scooped the world.

Niles Trammel, Vice President of NBC, Chicago, in the Merchandise Mart, was a big shot, you bet. In 1936, I had been canned in Minneapolis by a new station manager, and I went to Chicago on the strength of a letter written to Trammel by a St. Paul newspaper executive. You've heard how I hated that town. But now I again needed a job. NBC was cock of the networks. Powerful, forbidding and loaded with talent. In the Stevens Hotel (now the Conrad Hilton), I stalled around before calling Trammel's office. I was on the sixth floor; my heart was in the basement, and my hopes wobbled lower than that.

My call was answered by a woman with a bright, sincere manner and words that could have launched me onto Lake Michigan.

"Mr. De Haven, we've been waiting for your call. Come over and see us." A gift of new life for me. What a gift she possessed for handling people. I went to the Mart. I didn't meet her or Trammel. I auditioned, and I did get a job as emcee of *The Breakfast Club.*

So long after, I hope this secretary is well-rewarded for her deeds. This lady who said, "Mr. De Haven, we've been waiting for your call."

Merle Jones, a thoroughly nice fellow, was to teach me something I already knew, the meanness of big business. Jones, an Omaha lawyer turned CBSer, was sent to Minneapolis to obtain some seasoning as manager of WCCO. Okay with us mugs on the mike; we took them on in all sizes, shapes and ability.

During his reign, I was running wide and high in popularity doing *Friendly Time,* six nights a week, 10:30, half-hour, sponsored by Grain Belt Beer. Starting in 1943, it ran for eleven years, as I played current and popular records along with old timers. All music except for my talk and sound effects. At the show's opening, I poured water (the beer's sound in the speaker didn't sound like beer) from a Gluek (my sponsor's competitor) bottle — only bottle I could find for the first show, and it lasted eight years. An appetizing gurgle resulted; then I clicked the bottle and glass and uttered unctiously close to the mike, "Ah, man, there's real flavor — the flavor of friendly Grain Belt."

Now Grain Belt wanted to feed his show to a Duluth, Minnesota, station, and I had quoted a personal fee of fifty dollars a week to the advertising agency. Enter big, well-incorporated Columbia Broadcasting System, saying through Merle Jones, "We want part of this fee." Jones and I debated; off the mainline airs, people dicker for themselves, no agent. An engineer, he said, had to push in a plug to feed the show to the North and pull out the plug at the end. Does your imagination follow this? CBS wanted help in paying this engineer. Listeners listened to me, not Jones or the engineer.

Came the afternoon that De Haven was called to the showdown in the office of Mr. Jones. The exchanges come verbatim from the recesses of my memory.

"Bob, CBS isn't in this business to lose money."

"Nor am I," David slung back to Goliath."

"The New York office knows about this feed, and I have to report that we are making some kind of profit from it."

"I want my whole fifty dollars."

"How about one dollar of it?" Jones asked. Somewhere during his fight, Little David must have stopped to chuckle. Here I chuckled inwardly; I did pause, and I hope I smiled.

"You mean, Merle, that you and CBS will accept a fee of one dollar a week to feed six of my shows to Duluth?"

"That is the network's proposition."

"At a dollar, it is too cheap to pass up. I accept."

What does this prove? A dollar here and a dollar there, and, in a few decades, it piles up to fifteen or sixteen billions.

Jimmy Cagney. The New York theater knew him in the Thirties, and the movie world would soon know him as a box

Jimmy Cagney and Bob De Haven impersonating themselves. That mike was called a carbon mike and has not been used for about fifty years now. To put the movie gangster on the defensive I grabbed Jimmy's coat for the pose, and he froze as any actor would.

office smash. Warner Brothers Theater in Milwaukee bought to appear on stage with a movie release. The press agent steered him to me to appear on WTMJ. Jimmy and I shook hands and headed down a hall to a studio, but the actor took my arm and slanted me into an empty office. In a voice and manner as good as any of the hundreds who mimic him, Jimmy said, "Hey, tell me what I do when I get in that studio. I've never been on radio."

"Just listen to me and answer my questions. I won't throw any curves," I counseled. Our effort was well received.

Years later, watching Cagney strut stiff-legged and dance in "Yankee Doodle Dandy" on television, I casually observed to my wife that Cagney had learned a great deal.

Around 1940, John Cowles, Sr., red-eyed with fervor, led the Des Moines newspaper invaders to "serve Minneapolis" by buying the Minneapolis Tribune to establish a publishing monopoly. Our little radio station, WTCN, was not included in the bag. A bit later, a college chum of mine, Bill Steven, was imported as editorial boss. Bill easily discerned the double whammy delivered by the evenings Star's columnist and radio star, Cedric Adams. He wanted a duplicate for his morning Tribune. With Stanley Hawkes, a Cowles front office wheel, we lunched at the Minneapolis Club (where else to discuss a deal as big as this one?)

Thinking of the strict ban on liquor advertising that the new owner had brought from Iowa (you should see the booze bargains the paper touts now), my first contribution to the parley was to say, "You know, I'm sponsored by beer six nights a week on 'CCO."

"But you don't use your own name — you're called 'Friendly Fred'."

Hawkes and Steven allowed a small smile or two, "Oh, we know that," Hawkes said, "This has all been explained to Mr. Cowles."

We made a deal. I wrote the column. I lasted eight months.

Steven, this day of the long, long face, called me in. Accustomed to CBS gallantry, I was about to stretch on the rack to learn about the same quality in Mr. Minneapolis Tribune.

"We're in trouble," Steven announced, "John Cowles says you have to quit the night show sponsored by beer."

"John knew this situation before I started in the paper," I said.

"That's my defense. We brought that up to him, and his answer is, 'I must have been looking out the window when you told me.' "

"So?" I reasoned.

"I've done everything to save this situation," Steven confessed, "except to threaten to quit myself. The old man makes it an ultimatum."

My rattled brain functioned feebly to produce a thought.

On stage at the Minneapolis Auditorium during a Minneapolis Star
& Tribune Party. Bob and his three girls, Cedric Adams and his
three boys. 1945.

"There is an out," I offered, "I can quit the newspaper and
continue to peddle beer on the air."

"Yes, you can," Bill agreed. And that I did, and the
Newspaper Guild obtained severance pay for me.

In time, Steven's turn came to be canned. I asked him why
he was let out. Wisely he answered, "You don't win an argu-
ment with the publisher's son." In time, John Cowles, Junior's
turn came to be canned. I don't know what he said. I do know
that Steven and I had not cost the stockholders as much as the
publisher's son.

Dick Enroth is a fine man, serious-minded, an excellent
sports announcer. He worked the Minnesota mikes for years,
doing football, basketball and baseball. The Minneapolis
Lakers championship basketball team benefitted from his

work. Yes, the same franchise that is now at home and doing so well in Los Angeles.

"Slater Martin shoots from sixteen-and-a-half feet and makes it." Judging six inches on the floor from a broadcast booth might seem difficult, but not for Enroth. "George Mikan jumps to three-feet-ten and easily controls the tip off." Enroth coined words like the mint coins nickels. "The Minnesota center outstatisticized everyone else on the court."

One of the founders of the Brotherhood of Christian Athletes, Enroth does his good work with these men. Two family tragedies could not deter the man from his religious faith. Now he is a valuable member of the Billy Graham organization.

In his broadcasting day, his disinterest in any program except sports sometimes showed. At WLOL, he came upon a half-hour record program during his Sunday morning air shift. The engineer on duty told me that Dick was writing a sports story and had somehow started with an introduction of the second number on the list. Not hearing the first tune and probably not knowing one from another, he announced the third title and the second was played. Dick showed no awareness of the maladjustment but attended to his sports writing and remained contentedly one tune ahead.

During a showcase of WCCO talent in entertaining visitors to the State High School Basketball Tournament, Enroth did a half-hour in front of the studio band, giving the titles from a list handed him by the producer. Along in the middle he called off, in the right spot this time, "Now the band will play a popular song entitled, *Take The A Train*. He used a short 'Ah' instead of the long 'Ay.' Composer, you make take thee a roll over in thy grave.

Halsey Hall was the portly figure over there where the laughter came from. Sparse gray hair, pale blue eyes, the lower lip protruded slightly. With completely natural flamboyance, he labored prodigiously at sports writing, announcing and public speaking. His father was a newspaper man who took him to ball games; his mother was an actress and played with Modjeska. He was blessed with energy, and he blessed others with generous showers of goodwill and good humor.

Either or both of his writer-father and actress-mother could have given him the taste to discard the banal utterance or written line and substitute one with color, surprise or unexpected interest. Any pause in a Hall dissertation indicated his creative wheels were turning and would produce a bon mot worth repeating among broadcasting's bonest of mots.

On the baseball weather of the afternoon: "Well, the field looks okay after the rain, temperature about seventy, and the sky, I'd say (pause) is a sickly cerise."

For a baseball catcher, a low, short popup from the bat is usually a challenge; the ball looks so easy to get under and catch, and it ain't. One of these popped to the right side of Minnesota Twins catcher Earl Battey, who ripped off his mask, took two steps to find the ball already descending. In a violent action, he stretched horizontally to try for the catch and out. The little ball passed an inch too far away; it struck the rim of the mitt and fell to the ground. The catcher was "shaken up", as the announcers say; he brushed off the dirt as he arose and stood recovering from the fall. Halsey commented on the TV screen: "Well, if Battey would show a little hustle, the Twins mght have a chance to win this game."

Heights horrified Halsey; a life on the flattest Kansas plain would have suited him perfectly, and no steps or elevators, please. This phobia he reasserted one football fall from the top of the University of Washington stadium in Seattle, in a press section remodeled and enlarged since his last visit. A local newsman visited the WCCO booth to explain that the body of water to be seen to the West was Puget Sound, not the Pacific Ocean, as a network talker had referred to it the Saturday before. Hall opened the broadcast with a few compliments for the improved football palace and the newer but more elevated press and radio accommodations.

"I've just arrived at our 'CCO booth, folks, up about five thousand steps from the field (I started about one-thirty, your time back home), and my eyes are greeted by a magnificent sight, this wonderful West Coast — and high? Looking to our right, I can see, this year, a spectacular sight — the Indian Ocean."

Hall's position at the counter of the booth was beside Enroth, the play-by-play man. On the other side sat "The Grey Eagle" the unsmiling, newly-retired legend of football, Coach Bernie Bierman. (A friend of mine once characterized Bierman's radio commentary as being so dry he constituted a fire hazard in the concrete stadium.) Enroth would flame-throw his crackling play-by-play, stopping occasionally for commentary by saying abruptly, "Bernie" or "Halsey," a request for comment. One Saturday, I was listening, when a news flash about a car crash with four dead was handed to Enroth, who, with alacrity and no change in feeling or attack, read the copy then snapped, "Halsey...."

Mr. Hall slowed the pace with his first two words, "Well...now, " and with a trace of resentment he added, "What am I here? The mortuary announcer?"

Cigar smoke and the aroma of green onions (which he had been told would ward off cancer) were never missing in the small baseball radio booth he occupied with Herb Carneal and Ray Scott. As in the city room his trademark was booming, joyous laughter that rolled on and on. This happiness in sound took off without let or hindrance one night at the ballpark after Scott's nose gave warning about the state of the broadcast booth. Smoke and flames were rising from the floor under the counter that held their equipment. The ensuing chaos was explained for listeners by the other two; Halsey only laughed. His cigar had set fire to newspapers on the floor. "For the Twins in the sixth, no runs, two hits, no errors, one fire."

Six nights a week on WCCO-Radio, Halsey did sport news at 10:25. Live? Yes, we showed up in those days, no taping or filming, as live as the clock's tick and its tock.

After preparing the records for my show at 10:30, I usually killed time in the newsroom where Halsey was piecing together his notes. Most of the stuff was in his head, such as scores, percentages, schedules, predictions. Once from a remote broadcast in the fishing country up North, he had already started the feed of his five minute report. From

Minneapolis came word to use Halsey for fifteen minutes. Only a pencilled note placed in front of the veteran was needed. Halsey filled the time with items and opinions. We could freewheel then.

On another night I entered the newsroom about 10:20 to see Hall standing with his face against one wall directly under a loudspeaker that carried, from another station, the last seconds of a Laker basketball game. Applause and cheers swept in when the Lakers tied the score and the gun fired.

No cheers from the man listening in our newsroom.

He was standing there waiting for the final score to use on his sports program; running into overtime did not suit his purpose. From the old Hall burst a scarlet river of epithets and insults that, for artistry, would reduce a mule skinner or a drill sergeant to describing the three-legged race at a Presbyterian picnic. The expulsion of emotional torment caused a variation of the normal stance of a man looking at a wall. His feet did not leave the floor; they only seemed to. His thin hair fluffed over his eyes, and the cigar stubbed against the wallpaper. Hot words, curdled by profanity, fought for freedom through his snorts and gulps and coughs.

"I'll be goddamned if that sonofabitchin' game of basketball isn't the...God damnit, that's the crookedest game the Almighty ever permitted to be invented or I'll put in with you. The game should be over, and the Lakers should have won. Son of a bitch, how do they signal when the tying basket should go in? It's the goddamndest legerdomain since Blackstone's disappearing elephant demanded more money and Sunday's off."

Then he glanced at the second hand of the wall clock, pulled his unravelled emotions together, ignored me and the others, clanked down the hall to the studio and slapped the news of the Laker overtime on the air.

On one side of Loring Park on the Southwest edge of downtown Minneapolis, stands a statue of a famous Scandinavian violinist, one Ole Bull. Early in this century, his playing and concertizing were as beloved as his down-to-earth given name. In the park, Ole is drawing his bow in perpetuity across the bridge of his instrument. Ole did not go unnoticed one winter's night when the temperature sagged to fifteen below. Halsey Hall went on the air for his sports which he preceded with a weather comment, "Cold out tonight. So cold I noticed coming down here that Ole Bull had dropped his violin and put his hands in his pockets."

Near the end of his career, he was honored with an appreciation reception, dinner and program. Two thousand people filled a hotel ballroom to hear tributes from citizens and sports celebrities from town and around the country. Those on hand glowed with love and appreciation of the honored guest, and I, in a far corner, wondered how this wit could counter the accolades when he was called on. At eleven fifteen, Ray Scott introduced Hall himself, who broke his silence, after blowing a tornado of cigar smoke through the mike.

"Good evening, folks. (Pause.) About three months ago, when I first suggested this appreciation dinner...."

At the same affair a colleague repeated and authenticated the best known Hall anecdote. Stew MacPherson of Winnipeg retold Hall's numbing fear of heights and of air travel and to describe the man's dilemma caused by the assignment to football in Minneapolis one Saturday and a World Series baseball game in New York the next day. A train could not carry him in time for the Sunday date. The torture of a plane ride seemed inescapable. McPherson had found Hall fidgeting and snorting in the station newsroom and asked what his trouble was. Hall confessed. MacPherson tried to pursuade his friend.

"Come on Halsey, fly; live a little; make a decision. I'll go with you to buy your ticket."

The two of them walked the two blocks to the airline ticket office. At the counter, Halsy said in a shaky voice, "I want to buy one chance to New York City."

A WCCO Album

"As I remember, the question about this photographic effort concerned the rickety platform we stood on. Would it hold together until George Miles Ryan snapped the shot? It happened in the late sixties." Bottom row: Paul Giel, once WCCO Sports Director, now Athletic Director of the University of Minnesota; Charlie Boone, present day announcer; Bob Allison, a broadcaster after his baseball days with the Minnesota Twins of the American League for whom he starred in the 1968 World Series. Second row: Ray Scott, all-sports announcer, local and network; Dr. E.W. Ziebarth long time faculty member of the University of Minnesota and once Interim President of that institution. He acted as Educational Consultant for WCCO for many years after getting his start reading poetry on "The Red River Valley Gang" program; Jim Hill, farm broadcaster. Third row: Dick Enroth, sports and newsman; Joyce Lamont; Bob De Haven. Top row: Arv Johnson, State Capitol reporter; Sid Hartman long time Minneapolis Tribune sports columnist and sports commentator on WCCO; Howard Viken, still going strong as an announcer.

(Above) On stage at the WCCO Auatennial broadcast, Bob Hope seems to be asking for the hook for Bob De Haven. In the middle, Arthur Godfrey seems to want to strum the ukelele and sing. Big time radio guests enlivened the annual festival, rode in parades and met their fans face to face. Good times and good shows were had by all. The hey day for these productions was in the 1950s. (Upper left) Godfrey, De Haven, and Cedric Adams in the Aquatennial Parade. White sidewalls, yet. (Lower left) The Murphy Barn Dance, sponsored by Murphy Feeds, played for years on WCCO. The line up for this part of the Aquatennial blast, left to right: Cedric Adams waiting to say something; Bob De Haven saying something; Arthur Godfrey looking for something, probably the exit; Bob Sutton, station Program Director; Ernie Garven, accordionist and vocalist; Dick Link, bassist and vocalist.

Janette Davis, a fine pop singer with Godfrey, on stage at night after riding in a rainstorm with the same De Haven in the afternoon parade.

(Opposite) After he fathered three girls, De Haven disappointed his friends with the fourth child. A boy! The public wanted a fourth girl to match Eddie Cantor's famous four females (at that time). Maybe Cantor wanted and a boy and never let on.

(Opposite) Two guests of hundreds who appeared on "De Haven's Date" variety show, El Brendel (above) and Mischa Auer (below) of the movies.

(Below) "Mildred Bailey, a jazz singer of the immortal type and Ramona Gerhart Sutton at the piano. Mildred didn't remember our first broadcast in the early thirties; she was with Paul Whiteman's Orchestra and I was announcing for WTMJ, Milwaukee."

L_T

September 29, 1966

Dear Bob,

      *I thoroughly enjoyed being on the air
with you and with Joyce too.*

      *I like the way you handle your show.
And, I'll not forget that the name is "Bob"!*

      As they say in Arabia:

      May your shadow never grow less!

Lowell Thomas
Hammersley Hill
Pawling, N. Y.

(Opposite) Lowell Thomas, pioneer news broadcaster, Joyce Lamont, and De Haven in 1966. "Lowell was a gentleman and a pleasure to work with. Joyce, in addition to her many duties at WCCO, provided many of our fringe benefits. In this instant (above), another birthday cake for me."

(Above) Jim Hill, WCCO Farm Department, and De Haven in action.

(Upper left) Former Minnesota Governor and U.S. Secretary of Agriculture, Orville Freeman, Bob De Haven and Maynard Speece. The lady is unidentified. Probably a radio fan.

(Lower left) Governor of Minnesota, Elmer L. Andersen, answered questions of the radio audience directly from his office in the Capitol. He is on right and De Haven on left, wondering what to do next.

(Upper left) Heating up the WCCO airways at 8:45 A.M. for Occident Flour. At the table sit Jeanne Arland, singer and pianist; Burt Hanson, singer, and Bob De Haven. Peeking through from the guitar is Kenny Spears. These and other staff musicians and vocalists made the programs original and distinctive. Their shows gathered listeners by the thousands. (Lower left) Hard at work, Bob kisses Miss Fergus Falls on her arrival in the city in 1948, only yestderday. (Below) "We went right out into the country to broadcast from farmland. State and federal conservation departments sponsored plowing contests called Plowville, at a different farm each year. The Red River Valley Gang, Ernie Garvin, Hal Garvin, and Dick Link, showed up to go on the air and entertain. I, of course, came to show off my new sport coat."

(Upper right) What will this cutup, De Haven, do next? Perform an act of magic? Lead a parade? Return the hat and cane to a costume house? No, he is merely about to go on stage at a children's show at the Church. 1956.

(Lower right) Sad hill billy songs have a hold on the radio audience. In this act, Bob De Haven was a little too sad. Look at the faces in the background.

(Below) "De Haven (center) holds sponsor's cake mix in his right hand while comforting a donkey with his left. This ambidexterity doesn't impress the other donkey. Perhaps, he is either camera shy or embarassed by the proceedings. The spot is just east of Shakopee, Minnesota. Publicity, oh, publicity!"

Ribbing, kidding and roasting attained their zenith in WCCO's annual Christmas party for employees. No broadcast of these affairs. De Haven wrote most of these shows. Here the TV program "This Is Your Life" was parodied with a dramatization of E.W. Ziebarth's junket to Sweden. The cast (above left) did not hide their enjoyment of the proceedings. Second from left — Burt Hanson, singer, then Jim Borman, News Director; Jim Hill, Farm Department; Maynard Speece, Farm Director; Val Lindner, Program Director and, seated, Halsey Hall. The actor at far left is Clelland Card, impersonating a Swedish school teacher who seems to protrude in front. Best line in the drama of Ziebarth's peregrinations came from Card: "Ya, I met a fella named Doctor — a doctor? Doctor E.W. Zee-bartt, what did he pretend he vass? Educational Consultant of WCCO? Hmmm. (Patting his abdomen) Val, education vassn't what he was consultin' me about!" (Above) Even the WCCO brass relished the show. Left to right — look at Bob Ridder trying to laugh and eat at the same time. William J. McNally, then President of the outfit, risks a smile. Bob De Haven stands at the mike, his verbal cat-o'-nine-tails on the ready. Larry Haeg shows he is a sucker for a joke. Francis Van Konynenberg gives a haw-haw. In front of the table are Dick Stuck and Hartley Forrest. (Lower left) Burt Hanson emits a Swedish hill-billy ballad.

— 89 —

(Upper right) When Cedric Adams talks, everybody listens, including former Governor Harold E. Stassen, Bob De Haven, and Arthur Godfrey. 1948.

(Lower right) Joyce Lamont and Bob compliment Del Stanley of Dayton's Interior Design Studio on a job well done. Del and wife, Kitty, supervised the furbishing of the offices and studios of WCCO Radio.

(Below) Maggie Healey, secretary to the radio time salesmen, auditions the Christmas party emcee for a part in "Flying Down to Rio."

(Left) Packages of Butternut Coffee key-strips sent by readers in response to the sponsor's offer to buy gifts for poor children. Butternut Coffee and Standard Oil co-sponsored Bob's 7:15 A.M. news broadcast for fifteen years, beginning in 1950.

(Below) "Kids are a wonderful audience. These youngsters were in a ward of the Sister Kenny Institute, Minneapolis, where they were treated for polio. 1947.

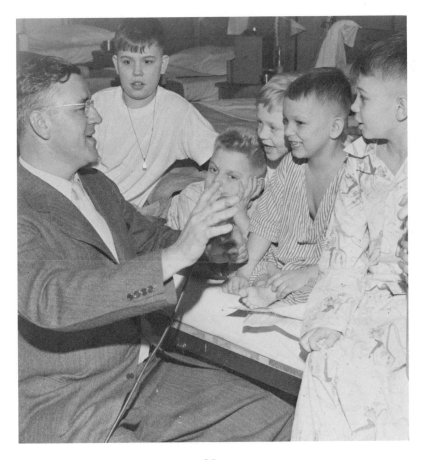

(Left) "A Dixieland dance in our own home was the bright idea of 1953. The band alone filled the livingroom. The host (Old Bob) danced with Honey March of Tulsa until her husband protested. Cora Christensen, tested a Middle C on the cymbal."

(Below) Our Hero here tells the cameraman how it feels to be married fifty years. Lookers-on are Madelaine Gilbert and Bob Wood who dropped in from upstairs. 1983.

In the WCCO master control room, looking wise and comfortable. As for the mysterious buttons and knobs, he wouldn't know which one to turn to draw a drink of ice water.

*　　*　　*

Paul Aurandt exhibited the brashness, noseyness, energy, ambition and the grace-saving good nature of most teenagers. At KVOO in the Philtower, Tulsa, he chummed with the musicians, announcers and engineers all of whom kicked him around verbally, which the young man lapped up. His manner was brisk and kinetic; his face long, blonde hair needing scissors.

His mother, a widow, was raising him successfully, sending him to high school a few blocks from the studios. Paul's vocation, avocation and recreation was trying to become an announcer on our far-reaching 25,000 kilocycles. At the time, a national headliner was the CBS news star, a Britisher named Boake Carter, who, strangely, sounded on the air like a Britisher. Paul took to impersonating the Carter style, "This is Boake Carter speaking," and to imposing the lingo on people around him. Once was enough. His burp was recognizably London. Paul was good, but he had then only this one act. A British accent in Oklahoma yet?

Aurandt made the staff, after I left, and went on to other stations. He wrote me from Kalamazoo, Michigan, about a fiction story he was trying to sell. Then Chicago — the same town I have been running down — picked up his unusual announcing style and started him to stardom. In his clipped speech and surprising pauses, his expertly written news entertained and informed. Television's appearance did not kill this hard worker in radio. Last time I heard from him in a letter, he advised, "Lay off that Boake Carter stuff."

Aurandt's name tag now reads, "Paul Harvey."

Along came Takayama Gizo. In 1960 and 1964, Mrs. De Haven and I headed tours to the Orient. They were sold on the WCCO air and called "Good Neighbor Tours" after a radio program of mine called *Good Neighbor Time.* Second time out, our promotional name was taken seriously by a Brotherhood of Roman Catholic clergy in Japan, one of whom had gone to the Orient from St. Paul. This priest proposed to the Kyoto Chamber of Commerce that the organization host a dinner of honor for us Americans. The Chamber accepted and we accepted this pretty high flying event for the people from Wisconsin and Minnesota. All arrangements were made to dine at another hotel, busses included.

However, events started to threaten our celebration of amity. The morning of the dinner, our priest-friend telephoned me. "We got trouble, Mr. De Haven. A Japanese student has stabbed Ambassador Edwin O. Reischauer. The dinner has to be canceled — I'll call you back after an emergency meeting at the Chamber office." The hands across the seas were pulling back.

By noon, developments took on a brighter aspect. The dinner would be held as planned without the presence of the Mayor, one Takayama Gizo, who was "terribly embarrassed," had lost face because of the stabbling of Reischauer and could not possibly face the Americans."

Matters would worsen if we officially pulled out; our feelings were not totally damaged; so we piled into the bus, sixty strong, and drove to the other hotel. In a small space next to the second floor dining room, I was directed to a handsome Japanese about five-feet eight-inches tall, broad shouldered, sitting with a handsome Japanese lady. She was the secretary and interpreter for the man who was the Mayor. She spoke in proper, pleasant English.

"Mr. Gizo asks not to attend the dinner in your honor, but he decided to come to the hotel because he very much wants to meet you and greet you. His is so sorry about the terrible action against your Ambassador that he cannot speak." Mr. Mayor did look dejected. We shook hands and bowed.

In the banquet hall, Kyoto businessmen were placed at

each table with our tourists, all smiles and goodwill from both nationalities. As we were eating, the Mayor and secretary entered to a smattering of applause from the surprised Japanese and took the chair at the speakers' table.

The lady explained to me, "The Mayor cannot resist coming in, but he will not address the dinner." Oriental reserve was slightly loosening.

The priest acted as master of ceremonies at the mike in greeting us for the Chamber and introducing the people at the main table. I responded through an interpreter, a means of communication that gives the interpreted a pause to think of what he will say next.

A few more items on the mike and then a whispering between the priest and the secretary. The Mayor would speak — only briefly.

The little man gave us a Chamber of Commerce welcome, made genuine by his chastened manner and warming words. The message: He felt almost mortally embarrassed that, during our stay, a Japanese student had tried to assassinate the American Ambassador. He found no words to right this awful wrong. Forgive him for not remaining for dinner.

My turn again at the mike. An arresting realization stirred my adrenelin. Kid, your not on the air doing something easy like selling breakfast food or describing a routine double play, shortstop to second to first. You are about to speak for the United States of America in a sticky situation that involves another country and the patriotic emotions of a worried political leader. You didn't audition or rehearse. There's the mike, and the audience is in plain sight. Uncle Sam needs you.

I ad libbed words close to these: "No American here charges the Japanese government or Japanese people with a dishonorable act. We remember with keenness and sadness the misery of one citizen senselessly destroying a national leader. In short and gruesome memory, we again see our President John F. Kennedy shot down and killed in Dallas, Texas. We know; we feel; we feel for the Japanese tonight. You are our friends in sorrow."

I must have said more; I hope I did not. Anyway, the

reluctant Mayor ask if he could speak again, and he did. This time with more ease and a hurrying smile or two. He strove to be what we called ourselves, a Good Neighbor.

After the party and back in our hotel room, the phone rang to announce a visitor in the lobby. She was the smiling Madame Secretary, thanking me for the evening (me?) and giving me a gift from the Mayor himself, a very large, illustrated book, printed in English, about his city of Kyoto, autographed in Japanese — Takayama Gizo.

Chapter Seven

Very little, if no help at all.

—*Heard on air, 1982.*

WITH A MIDDLE NAME such as the Russian composer below, I, too, might have stumbled into international fame.

Piotr Ilyich Tchaikovsky was born in Votkinsk, district of Viatka, May 7, 1840. I was born at 305 West Tenth St., second floor, second door to the left, in Anderson, Indiana, May 22, 1908. (You can look it up.) Antal Dorati, symphony conductor, was born also, about ten years before my date. We three came together in Christmas week, 1953, at Northrup Auditorium, University of Minnesota, for what, as events proved, was a stunning performance.

A shorter version is: The show was a hit and repeated annually for ten years, after which a dance company replaced me and my acting as narrator.

Antal, then director of the Minneapolis Symphony had an idea of staging a pop concert, using the *Nutcracker* ballet music with a voice telling the story. The job of asking me to perform trickled down to Old Bill Steven, my editor-friend, and I answered, "Sure, this is a way I can do something for the Symphony." This became an important "something" for the kids and their parents at the hallowed time of Christmas, and, for the Orchestra, it became a gorgeous fowl that laid golden eggs in the box office cash drawer.

Antal and I met at his home and proceeded to his piano room on the second floor. There was nothing like a script in sight, and I did not see narrating a ballet as an ad lib job. At the grand, the maestro noodled Tchaikovsky, loudly speaking the action of the ballet; music and words were news to me. I started to take notes on the back of an envelope.

This production was first performed in 1892 in a turmoil of artists, which sometimes burst into warfare. The composer (from this distance easily the most important of the bunch) became wretchedly owly about the story, which was a French adaptation by Dumas of a Christmas fairy tale, originated by a German writer, E.T.A. Hoffmann. Mario Petipa, master choreographer of the Imperial Theater, St. Petersburg, Russia, demanded that the music fit his dance creations. Other annoyances and frustrations attended the birthing of the classic, but they were all, by acclamation, put aside after opening night. Tsar Alexander III, when he saw the premiere in December, 1892, soared with delight at the entertainment as most Tsars and ordinary people and kids have in the following ninety-three years.

However, a show handicapper in 1953, seeing the pianist and a radio announcer at that rehearsal room, would have quoted our chances of winning an audience as remote as Votinsk itself.

After three hours together, I went home to put my notes into a version of a narration. Two days later we met in the same room. Dorati had no idea of my ability to write or narrate the story. Antal the Chance-taker — Bobby the Brave. We worked, trading ideas on the script and letting Piotr have his head with the music.

Gaining a chair (and a desk) in a symphony orchestra was a leap forward in my stage experience. Euphoria was immediate with ninety-some players around me producing the magnificent sounds of the magnificent melodies in the ballet, melodies that swirled around my head and went inside to remain. I had played many dumps and survived many dumpy situations before finding my chair just to the right of the Concert Master.

The maestro had marked his conductor's book at places where he was to give me cues for my reading. On my copy I wrote such notations as "Three brass buildups to GUNSHOT" and "Soldiers exeunt left." Latin soldiers. And I marked the time of the musical intervals between spoken passages, some over the music, some not.

We stood at the ready in our white ties and tails, one holding a baton, the other holding thirteen sheets of paper. In the wings, Dorati smiled at me and asked, "Are you scared?"

"No — never been scared. I am a little nervous, which makes for concentration."

"Right."

Walking between the violin section and the footlights, we received applause — for nothing, I guess. I sat down, looked around the hall, which held four thousand people, a sellout. My story would be improved here if I had mumbled to myself, "You've come a long way, baby," but I didn't think of that.

Then I started to read — cold, as they say, with no music. A newspaper critic called my vocal manner "avuncular." (I could have looked it up, and I did.)

Today we shall hear a Christmas story set to music, a Christmas present from our musicians and their conductor to you youngsters, all of you, of 8 years and 80 years and in between.

MUSIC: Overture — Waltz of the Flowers, 1 minute.

The waltz swept us off to a grand beginning, as the audience surrendered to the melody from the head of the crabby composer with the funny middle name. The music and reading brought to life in their imaginations a Christmas Eve in Nuremburg, Germany, at the home of Judge Silberhaus where the gift of a nutcracker causes a little girl to dream of Fairyland. We didn't name here because we hoped that every little girl listening would put herself in the story.

— 103 —

The second act brought the dances.

First the Prince and the Little Girl dance the Dance of te
Spanish Chocolates, the special ones you like the very best
of all and always eat first out of the full box.

And on and on through the story we moved, the audience
with us at every beat. Only a few rows were visible from the
stage; the kids wriggled, pulled at their parents' arms and legs,
but their attention did not wander. They jumped, then
screamed at the real gunshot ("This is WAR!"), which started
the fight between the Mouse King and the Prince. The Prince
won. In fiction, charming people win.

Then the finish:

(Mouse King to bows music — 3 minutes)
(After traveler closes, a big buildup to 4 cymbal crashes)
(Last speech cold.)
Do you know what? We have to stop dancing, but they are
still dancing in Fairyland, and they will never stop —
never in our imaginations — never in the whole world
and heaven — never.

What a line to deliver at the finish.

The applause was enormous in volume and enthusiasm;
the happy sounds crackled and smacked against the walls and
over the stage. We went off, came back. Dorati returned without me, shook hands with the concertmaster and beckoned the
other musicians to stand. He went off, and we both came back.

Critics were enthusiastic and predicted the concert would
become an annual event, which it did become with another
Christmas season. In succeeding years, we played the show, as
I have described it, adding a chorus from The College of St.
Catherine and Augsburg College. Dorati was tickled; his musicians, usually unimpressed, seemed impressed. The man in
the box office didn't look up; he was counting money. With
each new season, we added performances, and we ran twelve
years. A jarring annoyance bothered me, but, with the success,

Antal Dorati, conductor of the Minneapolis Symphony Orchestra, showing his "Nutcracker" narrator a few chords as they devise a script for the first of many holiday concerts. 1953.

I kept my silence: The lofty and famous Minneapolis Symphony, as a theatrical organization, gave us no help at all. No advice, no director, no suggstions. Oh, yes, a guy did check the speaker levels with the stage mike. He was an engineer. The maestro and I were the directors and the organization followed with the bows. Had we flopped, I'm sure we would have toughed it out all soul alone. That's show biz, to coin a phrase.

In 1961, Dorati departed, and Stanislaw Skrowaczewski walked on. Yes, a Polish iceberg can walk, compose music and direct an orchestra, you bet; but he does not need to have one iota of interest in a bash of holiday tunes and a narrator in a tradition that was originated by his predecessor. Stanislaw's cool rudeness to the show and to me was all right; larger problems than shoddy manners were needed to upset my stomach.

Before the first rehearsal, I introduced myself to him (the Symphony staff had no person to do this essential kind of work) and confessed that I was not a musician and could be sure of my mike entrances only by observing cues given by him. He answered in monosyllables, obscured by the mien and manner of an unhappy person wishing he were somewhere else, anywhere but on stage with a presentation featuring a radio announcer in a concert he had inherited.

After a ragged rehearsal, curtain time came, as it always does, and we dove in. I started my first speech on my own — after that — uncertainty. The new maestro missed a few cues to me; he was giving his attention to the orchestra, and I was the neighbor's kid who got in free.

Between acts I was annoyed, cool and wondering. Mario Andelucci, holding his oboe, came up to me in the wings and said, "You weren't the only one out there who didn't know what he was doing." Mario was referring to Skrowaczewski. Thanks, Mario. The second act went better for me and the audience.

Now Stanley himself is gone from our podium, indeed a gifted conducted, still waving that wand in Fairyland, forever and ever, I reckon.

*   *   *

Along came Max Winter.

On a sunny fall day, I was about my business, a sideline, of fronting for the radio industry by appearing at the downtown YMCA in Minneapolis before a group called The Christian Public Relations Committee. The other speaker and I were not strong attractions since only seven people, pens and tablets in hand, showed up to hear us. The other speaker was two-thirds my size, well dressed, smiling, genial, modest. He of the twinkling mind, one Max Winter.

At teenage, Max was brought to town from International Falls on the Canada-Minnesota border by his mother and father. On the North side of town, he scampered and scrambled for schooling and a living. On the Hamline University campus, Saint Paul, he stayed as long as his money lasted, a date that coincided with the basketball coach discarding him from the squad because of his small size. He and a retired and famous fighter, Ernie Fliegal, bought "The 620 Club" on Hennepin Avenue, a bar and hangout for sports people and politicians. He told me of Hubert Humphrey dropping in at the 620 after his first try and first defeat at elected office. "We talked a little, and I told him not to quit trying, and I gave him fifty dollars."

Things went along and Max bought a share in the basketball team and signed George Mikan to steer the creaky conveyance to three championships of the professional basketball world. Local owners sold to a Los Angeles group where the team is still The Lakers.

First on the YMCA luncheon program before the bulging crowd of seven, I listed the practical measures church people could use in feeding their news to radio listeners. This was about fifteen minutes long. The program became memorable after Winter was introduced. My memory dictates this version of his opening statement.

DeHaven here is well known, not me. I'm only a little Jewish boy from North Minneapolis who has ended up in the saloon business around the corner on Hennepin, and, frankly, it does my little heart good to make it here to the YMCA to talk to you church people. Thank you. To try to earn my lunch, which I have already eaten, I believe I'll tell you a personal experience of mine in public relations which has a title — 'How I got the Lakers into LIFE magazine'.

This tale he told:

Last winter I was in New York with the Lakers, and we were doing just so-so, in the game and as a property, and I was walking down the street and was asking myself about the Lakers and with no answer coming from anywhere, especially from myself, I asked the question again. What to do about the Lakers? Then the light bulb over my head turned on, and the answer came to me.

Get the Lakers a spread in LIFE magazine.

Our team would make good pictures and a good story. A story in a class magazine would rub some class off on us, maybe make the big towns think the Lakers and us guys running it were more than hicks who just happened to sign Mikan and were riding to the top. I could see that we were at a corner, and, if we didn't turn the corner, we would keep on being rated nobodies in the big leagues. Now, Max, how do you, smart guy, make the LIFE people listen to you story and write it up? I walked and kept thinking. Sometimes thinking will solve matters; this time it did. I had seen in the papers that, next day, the AAU (Amateur Athletic Union), headed by Asa Bushnell, was throwing another weekly football luncheon and tomorrow's was to honor Chick Meehan, football coach of Manhattan University. Another thought — a guy named Parker Vollers (not the man's name) was leaving a Seattle newspaper to become sports editor of LIFE. In a telephone book I found the address of the AAU and walked to the office.

I got past the receptionist by saying I had a grand idea for the lunch next day. I worked hard at selling my idea to the fellow she sent me to down the hall. My best line was: "I think I can get this Parker Vollers to speak at your luncheon tomorrow. He's coming to town to head the sports department of LIFE."

"We have speakers for tomorrow. The program is all set."

"No, not to speak. I mean just a few words, maybe only a bow. Look, the guy is new in New York, but you have him to introduce to the sports public here. You will be first. This could be a break for the AAU, and it won't hurt certainly. Maybe he won't come to your lunch, and, for that, why should he? But, if you give him three minutes, I'll try to bring him along."

"Three minutes then, only."

Then I went after this complete stranger, Mr. Vollers. I telephoned Seattle, got his wife and the guy had left for New York and was staying in such-and-such a hotel. Bingo! In five minutes I was talking to him on the phone. He hadn't been in New York before. Easy to see he didn't know enough about New York to cross the street, which was about all I knew. I told him I thought I could wangle a ticket for him to sit at the AAU's speakers' table. The guy was overcome; he couldn't thank me enough. He was so busy thanking me I couldn't thank him.

I went back to the receptionist and asked for two tickets and why. She gave them to me.

Vollers was presented at lunch. He did a two-minute speech. He got a hand, of course.

After the thing, we walked down the street to his hotel. He was still thanking me. We shook hands at the door, and I took fifty dollars out of my billfold and handed it to him.

"What's this for?"

"You don't think the AAU has speakers and doesn't pay them, do you?"

"Boy, can I use the fifty bucks with an apartment to find and a family to move here from Washington. Thanks again."

— 109 —

Maybe needless to add, the Lakers landed in a picture-story spread in LIFE magazine.

A player on the eighteenth tee at Oak Ridge, Max Winter's golf club near Minneapolis, used to face a small lake which lapped and gurgled almost to the tee's edge. On a day threatening rain, Max was finishing a round with a friend when the sky opened up. In the heavy rain, the friend's drive plopped into the lake as did Max's drive. Winter insisted on removing his shoes and socks and rolling up his pant legs in order to wade in to find the balls. Slightly annoyed and disappointed at the interruption, his partner drove the cart to the clubhouse.

Max was in the water when a lone female golfer appeared at the tee. The lone ball finder was not among her acquaintances on the caddy roster. She drove into the lake. Another ball — same result. She called to Max, "Hey, boy, I'm quitting. Find my balls if you can." Winter obediently toed through the water and retrieved her balls.

"Jump in," she invited and steered her cart to the clubhouse. There she indicated the rack for her clubs and pulled a half-dollar from her pocket and gave it to him.

"Thanks."

"Thanks," Max replied and went to find his buddy in the men's locker room to whom he boasted, "Look what I got, a halfa buck."

In those days that downtown YMCA sported a massage and steam room called the South 30 Club. After a couple of early morning broadcasts, I regularly went to the Y for handball or running and always a steambath in the South 30.

The steam room was soggy, hot, dark and small, room for about six people on the tiered benches on the sides. Past the heavy door, a visitor would stand in pristine nakedness on a forgotten level of Dante's hell. He felt wet, hot, imprisoned, forsaken, and he could not see because of the steam.

On this occasion, I was the entering man. I heard two chatty voices on the opposite side. Through the dark, I recognized one of the voices as Max Winter's. At the first lull, I opened up with a verbal attack, which I quote exactly: "If you

Jews would keep out of the Young Men's Christian Association, there might be room for us other people."

No hesitation in rebuttal on Winter's part. Instantly through the forlorn darknes and dripping murk came his spirited voice in mock anger, "De Haven, you son of a bitch!"

Mr. Winter secured a franchise for football in the National League, with some help from George Halas and others, and he named the team the Minnesota Vikings. During the season, he agonizes over his team's fortunes, and, off season, he recovers at his home on Oahu. His salary, as President, and his stock in the team keep him in spending money. Don't worry about this waif from International Falls; at Wailai in Honolulu and at Oak Ridge, he can always pick up some honest silver retrieving golf balls from the water hazards.

Chapter Eight

This is about the kind of weather you would expect on a
day like this.
— *Maynard Speece on WCCO*

My admiration for writers is without bounds. From the
writer's brain emerges the seed and script. Directors,
producers, actors, box office and literature all follow. Fred
Allen spoke it all in his defiance of ad agency critics of his
comedy script: "Where were you guys when these pages were
blank?" A mogul or a strawboss won't tell a cameraman how
to run his camera because he usually doesn't know himself.
Music is mysterious to the untrained; so the untrained let the
music alone. But writing — everybody has a pencil; everybody
has written a theme in high school; most people can read. In
writing there can be no mystery. Ho, ho. The moguls and
strawbosses are wrong, as usual.

A writer can be almost any gender, any height, in a beret or
bikini — any education, any combination of loyalties and prej-
udices and idiocies. He may sit still and think in an office or on
a mountain retreat in Canada, read Rabintranath Tagore for
solace and peruse microfilmed back issues of JUDGE magazine,
WHIZ BANG AND THE LITERARY DIGEST. He comes in all varieties of
normal and disturbing personality development. The writer is
a nut, savant, wastrel, perfect family man, dilettante, a bum.

But he is the home for a gift or developed skill of communicating the creations of his mind — a laugh, a philosophy, a wisdom about us sorry people of our planet.

Usually writers are not very entertaining at the Kiwanis meeting, the teachers' convention and the backyard barbecue. Their noodles are occupied with people you wouldn't know, situations that seem familiar but disturbing by being off focus. Usually writers don't talk well. Their product is acted, sung in lyrics, expounded from the rostrum, bound in books. The writer is the mystery. Everyone knows about the problems of growing old; one person, a writer, put them in a movie script, "On Golden Pond," an appealing story about old and imperfect people. (Someone in our family said, "My wife is in her second childhood; she waterskis on Golden Pond.") Robert Browning, the last century, knocked off a poem, longest in the language, and titled it "The Ring and the Book." And what is it? A mystery story. William Shakespeare could frighten the doublets off his Globe Theater audience in London, inspire them to a pandemonium of patriotism, wilt them in the tragedy of star-crossed lovers. Bill was a working stiff, and the next week the director needed to pitch another play into rehearsal. "Hey...Bill...!" Bill was also a genius.

For me, life has been easy because of the pleasure given by writers, and the comforting thought that there is more in print than one man can read in his lifetime.

Always wary, sometimes mean, I take a curmudgeon's approach to the blaring hype that precedes a "special" on the telly. On occasions I am wrong. One of these good specials was broadcast February 7, 1978 — a roast on NBC of Frank Sinatra. After almost switching away from the stupid porno remarks near the opening, I remained heartily to enjoy and applaud the artistry of the production. Abusive, put-down humor is tiresome, unless handled with a lilt and an assurance of underlying goodwill. Even here good writing saved the performers, the roasters who were getting laughs with every line. Even those I don't like I liked; Foxx, Rickles, Berle. All the way through I was thinking of the anonymous writers.

Gems: "When Sinatra moved from Hollywood, motel

sheets were flown at half mast."

"There's a small difference between Jews and Italians — just one grade in school."

"Columbus put it to Isabella, 'You got this wrong. The earth is round; you are flat'."

"Caesar, when stabbed by Brutus, 'There goes your Christmas bonus'."

"Bob Hope isn't here. He's out looking for a war so he can perform."

"They'll play golf with Burt Lance, but they won't let him keep the score."

"Sinatra, you bombed again. Dick Haynes could have filled this joint."

Jonathan Winters was funny that night when he posed as the truck driver for Sinatra's barnstorming. "Sinatra and 15 saxophones were in the truck. We'd stop at a town, and Sinatra and 15 saxophones would have their noses pressed to the windows."

After two hours, Sinatra came to the mike. "This business isn't easy. There are many hurts and disappointments. When I've been hurt, Dean Martin was the first guy there. Dean is not a drunk; he's not a fumbler. People are amused by that so he keeps on doing them. These people keep on joking, keep on smiling. They are wonderful. Everybody doesn't have to be funny all the time — Don Rickles proves that. Thank you. I hope you all live to be a thousand, and that the last voice you hear is mine. You receive applause, but not enough."

Nice speech, Frankie; I agree, and I include the writers. During the show's credits, their names were spun like a slot machine's lemons. So fast I can't recall a single name. But I did count. Twelve writers.

Sports announcers have no use for writers as they report the games of the world. They can't be saved from their abuses of the language, except, perhaps, by classroom instruction, and that must be out of the question. What mogul would spend a dime to improve the speech usage of his vassals? Also, the sports people are most amusing the way they are.

I heard a football announcer deliver this profundity in the

solemn voice of a prophet. "That quarterback has his future before him." So do I.

A pro hockey player was asked if fights in a game are for real. "If they weren't, I'd be in more of them." Now, that's funny.

From the baseball world Robert Proctor and Hal Higdon gleaned some lulus, delivered by announcers and reported in TV Guide.

"This young ball player at the plate has everything. The only trouble is that he doesn't often make contact with the ball."

"Reichardt is one of the few ball players in professional history who is minus a kidney."

"Seven years in organized ball — four in the minors and two in the majors."

"Richie Allen is an excellent base runner between the bases."

"I knew the ball was gone the minute it went over the fence."

"Swaboda gets a partial standing ovation."

"It is a long foul ball, but it was fair when it left his bat."

Jack Benny appreciated the writers' part in making him a super star. I first caught Benny on the stage at the Riverside Theater, Milwaukee. His hometown of Waukegan, Illinois, was nearby, where he was known as Benny Kubelsky, who was taking violin lessons, Meyer's son. (After Jack's fame developed, Meyer lived well in Miami, Florida, talking freely about his famous son to all and sundry. In a letter to his son, Meyer reported that everybody in the public park knew Jack Benny but one guy, "But who cares about him; he's only an old Jew.")

Benny's biographer, Irving R. Fine, makes it clear that Jack's climb to the top in comedy on stage, radio and television was realized through his own studious attention to his material and its effectiveness; young Kubelsky could get laughs, and he also could cerebrate and reason why — and why not.

He was one of the first to work with a team of writers,

using their output and making them judges and juries, along with himself, in deciding what went into a show. The team created characters to flow around the star, believeable people with rare qualities of amusement and action so that they wore well. They spoke carefully plotted lines, skillfully planted in the script to explode with the maximum effect.

The late Abe Burrows, a fine writer, said some writers "think funny." Comedy is the work of a genius, or, if that's too strong, the work of a rare bird whose mind jumps to verbalize a funny remark from the same material that another mind would draw the United Nations Treaty or a mortgage on a house.

Benny: "Now, when I played the Palladium in London, I was a big hit, just as Danny Kay and Bob Hope were. But somehow they did much better socially than I did. Danny was often invited to the Palace by the then Princess Elizabeth and Princess Margaret and went to many important affairs and parties with them. And Hope was very friendly with Lord Mountbatten and many a time played golf with him. Now those things never happened to me. Almost, but not quite. Once I was invited to dinner at Number Nine Downing Street."

Behind the mike a mispronounciation, an interchange of syllables or an unintended pun can charge the air with the electricity of disaster, or, if Fortune smiles, offer the chance for an ad lib that saves all. Writers do the same, using more time to make the repairs, of course.

Consider an occasion involving Mary Livingstone, Benny's wife and radio foil, and a simple, easy-to-deliver line: "My car was up on the grease rack." Mistakenly she read the line on the air, "My car was up on the grass reek." The audience roared and the cast broke up. Benny abused her verbally, declaring she had stumbled stupidly onto a non-word or two non-words. In subsequent shows, he castigated her for the mistake. The canny comedian and his writers were installing the ground work for a solid payoff.

This came in a show that originated in Palm Springs and closed with Benny interviewing the police chief of the town.

"Chief, have you had any emergency calls that were unusual?"

"Yes. Only last week we went out on a call. Two skunks were fighting on someone's front lawn, and, boy, did that grass reek."

Mary Livingstone jumped into the conversation to demand redress for the heat she had taken about the two words "grass reek." An instant apology was delivered by the humiliated star, made official by the presence of the chief of police.

Gag writers, it is said, seldom go out socially, even to lunch, and, if they do, they never talk. Once a gag leaves the mind and enters the air, it can be usurped or stolen. My hope is that this barrier is broken occasionally with the Benny writer-stars convening. The old laughs revisited would outdo most of what I hear today. Sam Perrin, John Tackaberry, Milt Josephberg, George Balzer. And Beloin and Morrow of an early time.

Benny delivered in perfect character the perfect tribute to his writers during the first of many air combats with Fred Allen.

Allen charged, "Benny, you could not ad lib a belch after a Hungarian dinner."

Jack responded angrily, "You wouldn't DARE say that if my writers were here."

*   *   *

Along came Mary Elizabeth Pray.

A Minnesotan enjoys a skill, developed over one-hundred-fifty years: he can perceive with invariable accuracy the difference between winter and summer. June, 1941 arrived on schedule, and I was very busy with the microphones. On Friday, Saturday and Sundy, I announced five baseball games played by the St. Paul Saints in Lexington Park. Indeed, my affairs were hectic that weekend. On the Saturday, the third of June, at Northwestern Hospital, along came the third of our three daughters, Mary Elizabeth Pray De Haven — a designated hit. And my wife adds that she herself had pleurisy the same weekend.

Lest I forget, also along came Helen, Heidi and John to fill out our siblings to four. Helen worked on the editorial side of the Minneapolis Tribune and Honolulu Star Bulletin. Now a housewife, she remains famous to me as the author of the line in a Honolulu story about a news conference: "One reporter remained, after the event was officially ended, laminated to the bar." Heidi married a New Yorker, a professor at Hunter College; she raises three kids and works in a law office. John is a family man and writes, edits, sells and travels for a publishing company. All three girls graduated from the University of Wisconsin. At this writing, their mother was out somewhere on her Harley Davidson and not available for a statement.

Rare photo of Hurricane Hat, her Harley Davidson motorcycle and her husband, Bob De Haven. Bob was allowed the driver's saddle on this occasion because it was May 22nd, his 54th birthday.

Chapter Nine

You have to screw your friends; your enemies won't let you.

—*Larry Haeg*

IN THE THIRTIES, as well as in the following two decades, the attitude of newspaper people toward us little broadcasters was always grudging and condescending. Oh, they might have conceded, under grueling cross examination, that an announcer would speak the correct time of day, provided he comprehended fifth grade English, that he could tell time if the studio clock measured six feet across for easy reading. Beyond that, imputing to an announcer the mysterious (to them) quality of news judgment constituted a waste of their own genius for imputations. There existed an easily discernable mindset in newspaper people (also now in TV news people) that they themselves are epic heroes on the ramparts where they defend the public's right to know along with their own right to profit by this bravery.

As an early broadcaster, you were an interloper aiming to stain their manufactured aura of holiness. Auras are reluctant to expand to include competitors.

A collision of concepts, early in my career, nearly cost me the friendship of a man I highly prized, a newspaper reporter and best man at our wedding. (As we approached the altar, he whispered to me, "I won't play unless I am captain and play first base.") To him I 'lowed as how the Charles Lindbergh family, after the kidnapping of their baby, had a right to privacy and, therefore, to protection from reporters and photographers. This fellow engaged me in a battle of protest, excoriation and damnation of my humane idea. I never had a chance; I retreated in disarray. What historians of journalism have decided about the treatment of the Lindberghs I have not had time to research. My mind is unchanged.

Standing on their constitutional right, blowing and bellowing, publishers and broadcasters mine their gold — in costume. Around their shoulders is draped a white mantle ("Et tu, Brute?"), bearing a laundry mark and a label reading "First Amendment:" they stand tall, by divine right, morally incorrupt and as obnoxious as most incorruptibles. In writing this, I am palpably unfair, but who observes the fairness principle?

The Chairman of the Federal Communications Commission (FCC), Mark Fowler, spoke to broadcasters assembled in Las Vegas, Nevada: "Your reporters and writers ... are better paid than ever. More talented young peole want into your business. Your technological news-gathering arsenal is awesome. To me it all comes down to three words: Get it right. Too often broadcast journalists are obsessed with getting it first, with confrontation, not coverage. Does the profession do itself any good to conduct a virtual stake-out in front of a public official's home and fling complicated questions as he leaves for work?" He also wondered what is accomplished by shoving a mike in the face of a grieving relative. "What's needed is not a bunch of governmental munchkins in the newsroom ... What's needed is responsibility by broadcasters' attention to detail, getting it right."

A first in the early Thirties was achieved by Bill Evjue of the Madison (Wisconsin) Capital Times in doing a daily morning broadcast from his office on his station WIBA. I posed as the announcer, sitting by on duty. (Under the 91st Amendment to the Constitution, announcers may sit or stand, as they elect.) Bill came on as honest and factual, reliable and well informed. One morning, he credited his daughter with correcting his pronunciation of King Tutankamen, whose final resting place was being invaded by scientists. War news, cats in trees, politicians in the State House two blocks away, a cooking recipe, a line on the weather — Bill devised the formula before broadcasting consultants analyzed the content of the news by laser and specified the haircut length and kind of smile necessary for maximum screen appeal. (If hairstyles change, you'll discover that TV news anchors have one ear on each side. Be ready.) Evjue was ahead of his time.

In 1931, in the metropolis of Milwaukee, we would grab the eleven a.m. edition of the Milwaukee Journal and read the headlines on WTMJ, plus a smattering of the best stories on page one. At the time, the Japanese were enlightening Manchurians by military invasion; the location of the war was the Province of Jehol — pronunciation, "Ray-hole,". Without radio editors and a backup of experts, we dumb announcers found out the proper way to speak the name.

By this time, the "EXTRA-EXTRA!", printed in tall headlines in a hurry and hawked on the streets in high drama was a lamented relic of the past. The flash on radio killed the extra on the street. I was one to lament. In my hometown of South Bend, Indiana, I had sold Tribune EXTRAS on the street with news of the first use of poison gas in war, WAR I by the Germans against the Allies at Ypres, Belgium. I also made the same run, selling confetti to celebrate the signing of the Armistice in 1918. Recently CBS-TV called this event "the Ar-MISS-tice." That ain't the way I heard it.

Back to the present, at about the same time as Mr. Fowler's speech, Jody Powell published a book, *The Other Side of the Story*, in which he related the years of trials with reporters while working with Jimmy Carter before and during the Georgian's White House years. Reviewing this book in the New York Times, Russell Baker wrote: "In Britain, where Waugh's view of the press, in his book *Scoop*, is widespread, reporters freely acknowledge their rascality and our First Amendment guarantees are nonexistent, press people live in constant fear of being judged for publishing material that annoys the government. The American press, by contrast, is a stuffed-shirt institution, overbearing in its earnestness, much given to sober self-examination of the self-congratulatory variety, and tiresomely asserting its rights. That these include the right to be unfair is a point not mentioned very loudly within the lodge ..."

Baker is critical of Powell's efforts.

"Powell cites only a few of the unfairnesses that galled him in the White House. About these he seems merely sore and anxious to set the record straight, which is mildly interesting but prevents him from writing with the sublime fury that the press's unfairness deserves ... I was let down. Maybe Powell is not the man for the job; he appears to be too much of a gentleman. He has let us off much too mercifully."

Turning the table is fun, and, once, I did this. By 1939, I was working for the fourth newspaper-owned radio station in my string of jobs. My nature was to be a good sport, thinking, "I'm the neighbor's kid in his backyard; you newspaper guys are entrenched; so you can bully me if you smile at the same time." On a Sunday afternoon in '39, I was home with the wife and two kiddies, not wanting to be about in the stormy weather that darkened our part of Minnesota. My wife's mother had sent a box of chocolate brownies — my favorites — and I had eaten two. (High drama always follows the butler bringing in chocolate brownies.)

The phone rang and the staff man on announcing duty at my radio station reported that a damaging tornado had struck and town of Anoka, twenty miles away. What do do? I carried the title of Program Director; decisions were up to me. I responded with the certainty of command and the lingo of those in power, "I'll call you back." Then I started pacing, looking at the sky from the windows and eating brownies to encourage my thinking. I threatened to go to Anoka; my wife cautioned me to stay home.

A week before I had met the operator of an air rental business. Another brownie — another phone call. I found my man. Yes, he would take me up for twelve dollars. Another phone call to my announcer to tell him what I was up to. By now, several deaths and severe destruction had been verified in the small city. I was off. Young Lochinvar to the West, actually to the Northwest. High winds and hard rain hindered my driving to the airport. Twice I changed my route because of trees fallen in the streets.

At the field, my pilot and I walked past an open hanger to reach his single engine job. In the hangar's open door, four or five guys were loafing. One of them called, "You goin' up?" My pilot jauntily answered, "Yep." The questioner merely shook his head negatively.

The tornado had smashed Anoka in a hell of wind, rain and screaming noise. Residences and buildings were flattened in a smash one-skip four-smash three-skip one pattern of nature's madness. A church, serving as an emergency hospital, was unharmed. A state mental hospital consisting of a central building and smaller buildings, was unharmed. In my air copy I wrote: "The mad storm took pity on others suffering from madness." A newspaper plane landed at Anoka's airport and flipped over before the photographer and reporter could get out. We didn't land; we looked and started home.

The brownies return to the story. I felt I had surrounded a bakery without the ability to digest a crumb. My immediate problem was securing my mother-in-law's cargo. The storm, trailing the tornado, tossed us around, and, over the Lake of the Isles, a slight accident rushed the climax. The plane's door on my side flew open; rain and wind swept in as if to claim the few square feet we occupied. Could I shut the door? Yes — with a struggle. Did I hold the brownies? Yes — Our Hero!

Our station was a proud member of NBC's Blue network, which meant that our highest rated program of the week was Walter Winchell's news Sundays at 8 p.m. which started with, "Hello, Mr. and Mrs. America and all the ships at sea ..." Our ship landed safely and I telephoned the studio with instructions, "Save the fifteen minutes after Winchell for me. I think I can make it with the tornado story."

Writing was easy, as I made much of the human side, death and loss, the careening plane, frail protection from the shattering storm.

Walter Winchell finished, leaving a maximum of listeners tuned to me. I went on the air for ten or eleven minutes, I suppose.

Right away the phone rang, a call from Dowsley Clark, Managing Editor of the Minneapolis Tribune, "Can we have that story?"

"Yes, if you want it," I answered, pretending modesty. His paper was half-owner of the station. I had to give it to him.

At home, I avoided the remaining brownies and told my wife the details of my adventure; she seemed pleased that I was home. The news scoop she was not much interested in. And the phone rang.

"This is Russ Wiggins at the Pioneer." (St. Paul Pioneer Press where Russ was managing Editor; later, he operated the Washington Post and now owns a paper in a small Maine town.) Up to this moment Russ, in his complete involvement in newspapers had given me only the required, "Hello." He was contemptuous of radio — then. "Bob, I guess you did what we should have been doing. Did you fly over Anoka this afternoon?"

"Yes, we did," I answered, conscious that Lindbergh used that pronoun, "We," to include his airplane.

"Someone heard you on the air and called me."

"Maybe someone did," I replied.

"Could we have it for the morning Pioneer?"

"Yes, if you can pick it up at my house; I have a carbon." What could I say? His newspaper owned the other half.

Next morning I had a front page by-line in both newspapers and little TCN had a scoop. (Brownie-eater smiles and flies into the sunset.)

*   *   *

Along came Roy Dunlap.

Some person, in the unmagic year of 1934, must have been an angel in disguise. In depression-abused St. Paul and Minneapolis, this angel has passed a tidbit of information to me. "That editor of the St. Paul Dispatch-Pioneer Press is from Indiana."

I took a chance on the Dispatch Building elevator, a see-through tube of grillwork and cables that was rated quaint three decades before and now was rated downright dangerous. On the second floor I opened the door marked "Managing Editor." There sat a big man, brown hair, portly, mustache, merry eyes, gruff voice. (No man speaking in a meek voice ever made Managing Editor.) Dunlap's later look-alike is the TV detective, William Conrad.

"What part of Indiana are you from?" I asked.

"Madison. Hell, come in, sit down. Who are you?"

We carried on easily and happily, talking about Indiana, radio, newspapers; in about ten minutes he sealed my trust with a quickie from down home, "The spelldown at the Church ended with a farmer and a monk being the last spellers, and the last word was 'hospice'. The farmer tried first, the monk second, and the monk won."

I sat there and listened to his story of Nina Clifford — a grand story which he enjoyed telling as if he were unravelling the *Arabian Nights* or *The Beattitudes*. And Roy starred in his own story.

Nina was the founder, owner and operator of a St. Paul house of ill and great fame. Hers was a flourishing business, well-known to men of several generations and by women who talked about it behind closed doors and flapping, folding fans. A college youth, upon identifying himself at Nina's, might be greeted by, "Come in — I know your father." In the netherworld of illegal love, Nina was St. Paul and St. Paul was Nina. The dashing, careless spirit of loggers, rivermen, still lived.

Nina Clifford died.

Dunlap received a phone call from Kansas City," I'm Nina Clifford's brother, and I live down here — been away from my sister for many, many years. I want her to have a proper funeral, but I can't handle the pall bearer selection. You, being a newspaper man, know everybody. Would you mind picking out eight of her friends and calling the undertaker who will do the rest and then that will be taken care of. Dunlap demurred for one one-hundredth of a second.

"Yep, I'll do that." Dunlap put a pencil to paper and wrote

down the names of fifteen St. Paul men and started to telephone them. "This is Roy Dunlap. Had a call this morning from Nina Clifford's brother ... you know she died ... he wants to know who her friends were ... he wants to ask them to be pall bearers for her ..."

Dunlap described the reaction: "I faced a Niagara of alibis — I could hear the mental wheels grind ... vacation alibis, going-to-Chicago alibis, family reunions in Wisconsin, mothers dying in Atlanta. With flustered gasps, everyone of these people claimed he had to be out of town on the day of the funeral. They were in panic. I brought about a hegira."

The editor paused to wipe his tears of laughter.

"Except for one on the list."

"Who?" I asked.

"Larry Ho. Good old Larry Ho. He said, 'Hell, yes, I'll do it. What time and where?'" Larry Ho was a by-line taken by one Larry Hodges, reporter and columnist, who was well known in the city and state and served as Mayor of St. Paul at one time.

Nina's brother came to St. Paul and found several pall bearers to help Larry carry Nina to her grave. Larry Ho — my newspaper hero of all time.

Chapter Ten

Play skillfully on the strings with loud shouts.
—*Psalm 33*

LUCKY I WAS; I spent three of the Depression years on Milwaukee. One day in March, I was paid, as usual, in cash, fifty hard dollars for the week. Franklin D. Roosevelt was busier than I; he closed the country's banks. How stark and sad was the debacle. Our sales manager at WTMJ said resignedly to me, "I think I can go to live in my brother's cabin in Northern Michigan. "Before the next payday, the same President opened the banks, and I was paid my next sixty dollars in cash, as usual. I lost nothing because I had nothing. Read that again aloud, if you can't make ends meet on $303.67 take home pay per week.

More in the way of luck for me were the stage shows that visited the town at admission prices I could afford. Second balcony at the Davidson Theater matinee came in at forty cents or about that. Two star-crossed lovers from Verona came to the theater, Catherine Cornell and Basil Rathbone in *Romeo and Juliet*. Part of the balcony scene I missed. Catherine I could hear easily, but my view of the Capulet balcony from the cheap seats was cut off by the proscenium arch. In the cast also was an actor, not from Verona, but from Kenosha, Wisconsin, sixteen years old. His name — Orson Welles. Why sure — the same fellow who unintentionally frightened the pants off Americans by a radio drama about an invasion of Martians.

Al Jolson was an overrated myth who couldn't be the star he had been created — or so I thought. "Show me" was my attitude in plunking down the price of main floor ticket in an insane splurge of money to see Al in *At Home Abroad*. The star entered from the back of the house, singing already; before he made the stage, the others and I were in his palm's hollow; he was everything I ever heard him called. Did he actually sink to one knee and sing "Mammy?" You bet, and he made his audience cheer. Years later, after he married Ruby Keeler he explained: "Some people say she married me for my money; so before the ceremony, I gave her a million dollars."

Late one day, after a matinee, I called on Fred Astaire who was starring in *The Gay Divorcee*, his first show without his sister dancing-partner, Adele. My purpose was to make a date for a broadcast on my show.

"What could I do?" he asked.

"You play the accordian in this show. Play it on the air."

"I can't play an accordian — I fake it out there."

"You could introduce your new dancing partner on the radio."

"Adele is the only dancing partner I'll ever have," he protested with annoyance. I gave up and said good-bye. But he did dance with another partner ... Ginger something ... Ginger ..."

At the Riverside Theater, I enjoyed a comic, unknown then and now, who greeted the audience with, "I'm certainly glad to be playing the Riverside Theater today; in fact, I'm glad to be playing any theater today." In the same house on another occasion, I laughed at old Doc Rockwell, a funny guy and a buddy of Fred Allen. Doc did a health lecture using a banana stalk attached to coat hanger as a model of a human skeleton. He stared through large, round and black-rimmed glasses to the spot his pointer indicated. "Now here the stomach is located. Believe this or not; one-half the breakfast food eaten in America is digested in the stomach — the other half is digested in Battle Creek, Michigan." Doc did come to the studio to be interviewed, and he was prepared with a product to sell. "Doctor Rockwell's Prepared Dandruff. Just the answer for people breaking into high society. When you attend a formal dinner where the men all have dandruff on their shoulders and you have none, pull out your container of my prepared dandruff, and, in an instant, you'll be well groomed like the other men around the table."

In our childhood home, our first automobile (5-passenger, 4-cylinder, wire wheels, Essex touring car) rated second in the notable events of two decades only to our acquisition of a Brunswick phonograph. The cabinet provided record storage space and put the turntable at elbow height, perfect for changing the pickup heads for various makes of records and for manning the crank handle that fit into the right side. The sound box was wooden, which "makes for perfect reproduction," we were told. What came out was good enough for me, even if it was perfect. We learned something of classical music and heard the headliners (Caruso) on Victor Red Seals and Pathe Records. The Dixieland route was my pleasure; Decca published Red Nichols at 25¢ per record, two sides, mind you. Well worth saving for. I can hum his arrangement now of the song *Ida*.

Remember? *Dardanella*; *Poor Butterfly*; *Hello, Central, Give Me No Man's Land*; *Oh, By Gee, By Gosh*; *Just a Baby's Prayer at Twilight*; *Yes, We Got No Bananas*; *Long Boy*; *I'll See You In My Dreams*. In the basement of the dime stores a twenty foot square displayed sheet music all the way around. Inside worked a pianist, a girl, who would play any selection on the piano that a customer wanted to hear. I stood some distance away to listen; I never had the money or the nerve for a sample. *Naughty Waltz, Home Again Blues, Linger Awhile*.

Early radio leaned to classical and semi-classical music in studio presentations; this show of good taste fed the infant industry. (And made me learn fast. When the soprano put *Londonderry Aire* on her list, I knew it was not the milk business in London or the derriere the French usually talk about.) Popular records, stations learned in the Thirties, had enormous appeal, and they became fodder to fill the hours then — and now. Fred Waring (and the Pennsylvanians from Penn State) sued the radio industry for a reckoning and payment on the use of his records. He lost. Caesar Petrillo called a strike of his Musicians' Association against the use of records on radio; Caesar won and lost, since he won higher fees at the recording studio, and the stations gained unlimited use of records with the purchase price.

In 1930, I was assigned the *Shut In* program on WIBA for people confined to their homes. A solid idea that worked. I aired at 3 to 4 p.m. In the early afternoon, I picked my records at Cec Brodt's Music Store on State Street, then drove in my brother's 1922 Dodge to the studio, just off Capitol Square and did the show. Seems I was one of the very first disc jockeys. Among my early favorites was Bing Crosby singing *I Surrender, Dear* with Gus Arnheim's Cocoanut Grove Orchestra and Johnny Green's new one, *Body and Soul.* After the show, I returned the records, paying a rental for the afternoon of 10¢ per disc.

The following year on the staff of big WTMJ, Milwaukee, I observed Johnny Olsen going on the Sunday morning air with "Masters of Rhythm," three hours of pop records in a program, predicted by most station people to be a failure from the start. From the start it was a solid hit that swept up the town's Sunday listeners. Olsen had come over East from my old WIBA when I tipped him off to the job opening. Yes, the same Johnny you hear and see on network radio and TV to this day. He became an expert at warming-up a studio audience and has never been out of work. His home town — Windom, Minnesota. When Johnny first landed at the Milwaukee station, he asked me for advice. I had the answer. "Do your shows as best you can and go home. Don't sit around and gossip with the talent or the office help." Olsen obeyed. Once we plotted to buy a station in Madison, South Dakota, a benign plot that rests now in some parched steer's skull on the prairie.

Radio played the pop music for you, and you loved that; no need to frequent the basement of a dime store. You and I attached our feelings and sometimes deep emotions to the words and music. Tunes were part of our lives. I'd hold

Carolyn's hand while driving that 1923 Essex and hum *I'll See You In My Dreams* — our song.

"One phone call and we're in," were my words in assuring my dear wife of better times coming through the magic of show business. Between Christmas 1942 and New Year's 1943, my call came.

"This is Ed Cashin." A Minneapolis advertising agency man.

"Hello, Ed, old boy, what can I do for you?"

"I'm looking for a man."

"Ed, people parade through my office every day looking for work on the air, and some of them are good. I can probably find what you want."

"I want you."

Zap! The sponsor was Grain Belt beer and the station, WCCO, the biggest in audience and prestige. I had grumbled to my wife more than once, "A guy could read page 394 of the telephone directory on 'CCO, and he would be a star." My air name was to be Friendly Fred because the product was known as The Friendly Beer, as Ed Cashin added, "Whatever that is." Fifteen minutes at ten-thirty at night, six nights a week, playing pop records I selected. Here came the capital letters — at ONE HUNDRED-FIFTY DOLLARS A WEEK!

Celebration at home was unrestrained. "Give me three weeks," I shouted, "and I'll clean up the Dayton (department store) bill." I had always loved records and had used them on other shows: my lingo and manner would fit into the nighttime to make the commercial pitch appealing but not boozy.

At the end of three weeks, Ed Cashin and the sponsor were not happy; if there had been an impact, it was small. Ed said, "Let's go to a half-hour with the format and see what happens. How much money do you want?"

"Two hundred a week," I said.

"Make it one-seventy-five."

"A deal."

Hardly noticed by listeners in fifteen minutes, the music and the mood of the show registered solidly over the longer route. I played records I liked by artists I liked, and talked to those sleepy night people in a few short sentences and phrases and let the music do the work. Six nights, half-hour for eleven years. I paid the Dayton bill and some others.

At the show's opening, I used a simple sound effect made by ater poured from a bottle into a glass. I wrote the opening on a piece of scratch paper and never changed the thing:

De H: It's Friendly Time!
MUSIC: Opening tune, non-vocal. Fade on cue after melody is established.
De H: Brought to you by Friendly Grain Belt beer.
        (pour water in glass)
        Ah, man, there's real flavor — the flavor of Friendly Grant Belt beer.

In my low, unhurried and sincere (yes, I showed sincerity — remember the Dayton bill?) voice, the "real flavor" lines was believable and effective.

A man about town, Joe Ferris, served as a Minneapolis Tribune reporter and, in Friendly Time times, as public relations boss of Northwest Airlines. Joe described to me an evening he spent at home alone; his wife and son had gone to Florida. Joe had called it a day and gone to bed to read. The radio brought in my "Ah, man, there's a real flavor" line. Joe turned off the light and tossed his book away.

"I became restless," he continued, "My eyes closed and opened right away. Your music started. I turned on the light and looked for the book. I tried to read — no use. I got up and dressed and went out to a saloon to get some Grain Belt. Honest I did."

There's real flavor and there's real salesmanship on the radio.

War II raged. Families and sweethearts were left behind, as nearby Fort Snelling (founded in 1820) shipped men out every day. The sentimental lyrics of the songs touched most listeners to make an emotional contact with someone absent. The listener filled in the name. I treated both the music and the audience with respect. All arrangements were played out to their ends, never a suggestive lyric or off-color comment. We used "Auld Lang Syne" by Guy Lombardo as a closing theme. Now you'll understand the pull of the show — Royal Canadians all.

The sponsor, the agency, the station were all pussy cats for over ten years. Frank Kiewel, President of the brewery, called me at the studio one night about 10:40, six years after opening night.

"Bob, this is Frank. I'm over at the Athletic Club with some friends, and they want to see our show. I've never seen it in the studio either, you know. May I bring them up now?"

"Sure, come on," I answered. I did not add, "Why you're the sponsor; after six years, you ought to have the right to visit one tiny, little Friendly Time."

The visitors enjoyed the backstage visit. Frank did ask why I used a competitor's bottle for the sound effects. I explained, "Just started that way and found that Gluek's makes a truer sound of Grain Belt than Grain Belt." Frank was slightly puzzled by this but accepted the explanation.

Pop tunes on the radio mark events in our lives. Some of these tunes will kindle your memories; so let's go on a binge; hum along and have a Grain Belt or a sarsaparilla.

Buckle down Winsocki, best of football rousers. Stan Morner, fellow announcer at WTMJ, became Dennis Morgan, the Warner Brothers movie star. In La Canada, California, one night, he took about eight of us to a restaurant for dinner. On seeing Dennis, the organist struck up *On Wisconsin*, Morgan's trademark. This night we were seated at a long table and I next to a fellow named Ralph Blane. Others in the dining room called out their college requests —U.S.C., Yale, Navy, California. The organist complied, adding *Buckle Down Winsocki*.

"That's my song," Blane said to me.

"Oh, I didn't know that's a real college song. Where did you go to school?"

"No school, but it's mine. I wrote it for a movie."

Blane's home town is Broken Arrow, Oklahoma, and he also wrote the songs for Judy Garland's *Meet Me In St. Louis*

— 133 —

which contained *The Trolley Song* and that wonderful song of young love, *The Boy Next Door.*

When I Take My Vacation in Heaven used to be sung by a cowboy group on WTMJ that was selling a product called Crazy Water Crystals out of Big Spring, Texas. This appealing ballad I never heard again in the fifty years between then and now.

My Funny Valentine, sung by Frank Sinatra in a Minneapolis benefit for the Presidential campaign of Hubert Humphrey. I attended, expecting to sit through some extended political palaver, the price of waiting for the music. No palaver. We delighted in the fine music by this high-spirited and sensitive vocalist. Near the end of the three hours, Sinatra stated quietly and convincingly, "I'm here tonight in the interest of Hubert Humphrey. I hope you vote for him." That was all! That's class! Argue, if you wish, that Frankie is obstreperous, ornery, self-willed — okay. He is the superb performer, also the one who once said, in a joust with "journalists," "All I owe my audience is my best performance." Neophytes, hang that on your wall.

Paddlin' Madelaine Home. For ten years, Joyce Lamont, a fine radio performer, and I aired a show on WCCO, 7:30 a.m., six days a week for the First National Banks of St. Paul and Minneapolis. I selected the records, and the bankers had ideas about the music also, as you would expect. Through the grapevine of banks, vice presidents, ad agency and station brass I was advised that a retired President of the St. Paul First National Bank objected to "Madelaine" because of an "obscene" line. "I'd kiss her and kiss her and then paddle some more." My reaction to the silly uproar was put into words, not used on the air, "Well, how obscene can you get in a canoe? It tips."

Tea For Two the tap dancers favorite. Hear the stops and shuffles? Frank Fay made a funny monologue from the lyrics by over-analyzing them. "Bake a cake for me to take for all the boys to see," Frank would recite; then a quizzical voice, "Now what would those boys really say if I took a hunk of cake to the gang in the boiler room and offered to divide it?" Fred Allen's remark about Fay is too choice to leave out. "Frank Fay was last seen strolling down Lovers' Lane, holding his own hand."

Shake Hands With A Millionaire. Radio carried it in the Depression's darkest nights, the simple story of a guy who spends the day looking for a job — no luck. Defeated and discouraged, he comes home where his kid runs across the yard and yells, "Daddy." The song flows into the refrain, "Shake hands with a millionaire." Corny? You didn't hear it when I did in 1933. Later, my own son was jobless, and I told him about this song.

Rudolph, The Red-Nosed Reindeer. Scene: New York City, splitting hot summer about 1951. Chesterfield cigarettes brought disc jockeys from around the country for brief interviews on its summer replacement with Robert Q. Lewis, King Cole and Ray Block's orchestra. Yes, I was called. We rehearsed in a theater-studio in the afternoon. Rehearse? Well, we sat around for three hours. People were friendly. In the half darkness, a fellow in the row of seats behind me tapped on my shoulder.

"You're from Minneapolis?"

"That's right."

"How's Rudolph doing out there?"

I was supposed to know a guy named Rudolph?

"Rudolph who?"

"The red-nosed reindeer. I'm Johnny Marks, I wrote that song. How's he doing?"

The song's still doing well, particularly in December.

Is It True What They Say About Dixie? A fellow who had just given me a job as emcee of "The Breakfast Club" was showing me the NBC layout in the Merchandise Mart, Chicago. We stepped into the control room of a studio where a girl singer and a band were rehearsing. The girl was big time Chicago; chic, small hat, skirt, half-sitting, half-standing beside a tall stool. She was belting out this song. "Does That Sun Really Shine All The Time?"

She's Funny That Way. A proper and moving love song with poetic feeling. Oh, to be in college when proper love songs and poetic feelings were there. Joe Shorr's band played in Madison's Parkway Theater, and Jimmy Pettycord, a dropout, sang that song.

Daddy's Little Girl. When playing this on the radio, I would occasionally mention my baby girl. "You're the spirit of Christmas — the light on the tree." Molly, years later in her forties, signed a letter to me, "Daddy's Little Girl."

Thanks For The Memory. Hope's theme. On a long ago Sunday night, I heard an entertainment on radio of U.S. troops in Germany. Bob Hope was the comedian. On the following Thursday, he was in our town for a personal appearance. I lugged recording equipment to his room in the Radisson Hotel, and just the two of us did the interview. Standing at the door to leave, I said, "I heard you on the air Sunday in Germany. Does that travel upset you or tire you out?"

"Naw, nothing bothers my stummick."

Don't Cry, Little Girl, They Have Broken Your Doll I Know. My dad would sing this in a hammy falsetto to anyone at home, suffering from a supposed hurt. *The Prettiest Girl I Ever Saw Was Drinking Cider Through A Straw.* This he would sing anytime for no reason at all.

All of Me. A fine standard. In a nightclub, I renewed acquaintance with accordianist Art Van Damme. We had entertained soldiers at Camp Savage. Art and his group raced through this tune in that club to give his people a chance to display their amazing technique. When it was finished, Art spoke softly into the mike, "After playing that tune at an utterly ridiculous tempo ..."

That Rainy Day is a splendid song that tells the emotional story of a busted love affair. Jeanne Arland, pianist and singer, worked on many radio shows with me. Her husband, Willie Peterson, an accomplished professional musician, had died shortly before this incident. We did a special performance with a band and broadcast at the Old Log Theater, Excelsior, Minnesota. Jeanne was scheduled for *That Rainy Day*; as she brushed past me to reach the piano, she whispered, "I hope I can get through this." She did. The song ends with a phrase, "That rainy day is here."

Beautiful Doll. My first song in my first act. I was about five, in a white suit, dickey collar, slippers, Buster Brown haircut — my Sunday best. My mother played the piano and I sang this current hit. "Let me put my arms around you," and do something else that rhymed. I forget. I couldn't sing.

I Can't Get Started With You, by Cole Porter from Peru, Indiana. In our college fraternity house, the monthly dances were usually played by a five-piece orchestra headed by pianist Bob Berrigan, a genial, accommodating guy. Occasionally a chair was filled by his nephew, Bunny Berrigan. Bunny and his horn blew into the top of the New York music scene, and his playing and singing on a record of *I Can't Get Started*, is a classic, still played often on the radio. "Mrs. Roosevelt has asked me to tea."

I'm Gettin' Sentimental Over You. Tommy Dorsey took it as his band's theme song. The Boswell Sisters first sang it on a record, which I played on WTMJ. My best girl, a student at Madison, used to come over for the weekend — 1932. We suffered when the parting came Sunday evening at the rail station. This one Sunday, we said good-bye and I returned to the office to check some records. *Gettin' Sentimental* was coming through the speaker. Our song. In she walked and explained, "I can't stand going back to Madison tonight." We were married a year later, way back in 1933; we remain that way, up front in 1985. "I'm Staying Sentimental Over You."

Indian Love Call. Nelson Eddy wooed Jeanette MacDonald with this fifty years ago; he sang irresistibly in his uniform of the Royal Canadian You Know What. Even in the black-and-white movie his outfit and Smokey Bear hat were fetching. One winter's night in Arizona, I sat past midnight to see a TV rerun of *Rose Marie* and to hear Nelson sing this song. Gosh, He was good and old fashioned... Next evening in front of dinner guests, I became carried away in describing the Eddy performance and jumped up to imitate him. My smash impersonation received a thunder of applause and laughs. One guest asked me where I had studied voice. Studied voice?

Minnie The Mermaid is a simple ditty about love under water (not the most desirable place) that Bunny Lyons used to play and sing in college days. "Down among the corals/ She forgot her morals/ She was just as happy as could be/ And every night when the star fish came out ..." Some wag stated that Minnie failed in show biz because she couldn't do the splits.

Star Dust is most beloved by sentimental Hoosiers, and they all are sentimental. Hoagland Carmichael wrote the music; he was a Bloomington native and a graduate of Indiana University there, both gilt-edged Hoosier credentials. In his book, *Star Dust Trail*, Hoagy wrote about his first humming the tune during a solemn walk home after a quarrel with his girl. "Looking up into the trees, I started to whistle it ..." or some such reference. Much later, Hoagy played a Minneapolis Hotel (and the Edina Country Club golf course), and I interviewed him on the air. I referred to the current TIME magazine article on himself. "Hoagy, this TIME magazine tells one version of you writing *Star Dust*, and in your book you tell another, a different story. Which should I believe?"

"Now, Bob," he replied in his raspy and pleasing Southern Indiana speech, "Would you expect that TIME would know more about writing that song than the little ole guy who wrote it?"

Little Man, You've Had a Busy Day. Running around the WTMJ studios, looking busy, I stopped by a control room overlooking a studio that was on the air where *Little Man* was being sung. The engineer at the controls was one Harry Slipinski, nicknamed "Slip." I asked him some question, but he didn't answer; his hand tightened on the knob he was holding. There were tears in his eyes.

Brashly I said, "Don't let that song get to you, Slip."

He replied, "Wait 'til you have a kid of your own." I did wait, and then I understood.

Don't Worry About Me. Some of us went to the Minnesota State Prison to do a Saturday afternoon entertainment. The cons supplied the orchestra; we supplied about six acts from radio stations and night clubs. Near the end of the afternoon, I introduced Flo Seidel, singer and pianist, a cripple since childhood, smiling and friendly that day as she had been all her life. She limped on the stage and sang, *Don't Worry About Me ...*

I'll Get Along. At the end they gave her applause and cheers. She did two encores — little Flo and her smile and her limp, disabled as was her audience. The two of them understood.

Before I left the "Big House," the Warden thanked me for the show.

"Only one thing I'd mention," he said. "That song of Flo Seidel's. The inmates have many worries and the hardest one is worry about the wives and sweethearts on the outside. Are they picking up with another man? Next time substitute another song."

I've Got A Crush On You. A friend of mine touted me on Joe Sullivan, pianist, writer of *Little Rock Gitaway*, which was a farewell to his mother-in-law. We went to a night club-saloon down the Minnesota River. Out comes this jazz artist in a business suit and plays the piano for an hour. No talk — just music. "I've got a crush on you, sweetie pie."

Just a Closer Walk With Thee. Once I have been truly transported by song and singer — when, on a sad occasion, one Burt Hanson performed this spiritual. A finished artist, a wonderful song.

The Hills of Home. In Milwaukee days, Dennis Morgan, The Prince of Song (my name for him) and Myrtle Spangenberg, The Princess of Song (my name for her) were a duo knocking out the semi-classical hits. Get it? The Prince and Princess of song. Morgan would render *The Hills*, which he pronounced properly "Heels," as instructed by his vocal coach. If you telephone him today at his ranch home near Anwahnee, California, and ask, "Are you happy among the heels of home?" he would answer, "De Haven what do you want?"

I Got Rhythm. I was sent from Milwaukee to Madison to handle a WTMJ pickup of Paul Whiteman's orchestra at the University Junior Prom. First, I called on Whiteman, of the enormous girth, in the Lorraine Hotel to ask permission to make the pickup. He was in bed enjoying a massage. I thought of the wag who said that he knew a wren who had returned from a long flight from Whiteman. My request he refused. We sent up equipment anyway. That night I worked an off-stage mike beside the nearest musician on stage, the wonderful art-

— 139 —

ist, Frankie Trumbauer (*Singin' The Blues*), who gave me the title of each number as it came up. Whiteman started the dancing with the impact of a 21-gun salute, *I Got Rhythm* with Mildred Bailey on the vocal.

Easter Bonnet. Our first child, Helen, was between two and three years of age when we lived in Tulsa, where I emoted over KVOO. We lived in a basement, but with a radio you can bet. Helen picked up this tune and brightened our lives by singing, "In your Easter bonnet with the sweet potatoes on it."

On December 8, 1941, I stood in the Northwest corner of our Minneapolis living room listening to the radio and to Franklin D. Roosevelt. "Yesterday ... a date that will live in infamy," — the Japanese attack on Pearl Harbor. I did have a fleeting thought, as other program managers might have had. "What can the announcer say at the end of the address? How will radio drop a curtain on this historical event that stunned our people with blows of surprise, fear and frazzled hope?" Well, at CBS, they didn't say anything. At the end, a band played *The Star Spangled Banner.*

Someone To Watch Over Me. This love song has for years stood far beyond the banal in its Poetic yearning, in music and words, for a mate. Then I learned it is more than a love song from two musician friends, Larry Malmberg and Ovid Bastien and a third player. They were off stage at a last performance for a violinist and conductor, Wally Olson. Wally's funeral. They played *Someone to Watch Over Me.* A Gershwin ditty at a funeral? Yes. Appropriate? Oh, yes.

*   *   *

Along came two little old ladies.

A Wisconsin-Minnesota football game in Minneapolis gave me a chance to check the pronunciation of a place-name. I went along with a ticket that put me on the Badger side of the field. On my right sat two little old ladies. During the first half I learned from overhearing their conversation that they were well informed about the game. One of them said to her friend, "If Wisconsin goes to the Rose Bowl this season, I'm going out there. I wouldn't miss that game for the world."

Between halves, the three of us started to chat. As usual, I admitted to being a University of Wisconsin alumnus; they admitted they were from Lancaster in western Wisconsin.

"Oh, Lancaster. I'm a radio announcer, and we are supposed to pronounce the names of towns correctly. I know in Pennsylvania the town is called 'Lankas-ter'. What do you call yours in Wisconsin?"

"Both ways actually," replied one of them. "We use them both, maybe LAN-caster more often."

"I've never been there," I added. "Only thing I know about Lancaster, Wisconsin, is it's the home of the All-American end in the forties, the one who was killed on Iwo Jima, Lieutenant Dave Shreiner, U.S. Marines."

"Yes," the little old lady nearest me answered, "Dave is my son."

*   *   *

And along came Kenwood Plumbing.

Kenwood Plumbing
2107 Penn Ave. So.
Minneapolis, Minn. 55405
May 22, 1978
To Bob De Haven from the Kenwood Plumbers:
Happy seventieth birthday! We have been involved with the De Havens so many years we feel we are part of the family. I guess I remember Molly the best because she was always our helper and often said she was going to be a plumber when she grew up.

We note some of the most common problems you had when living on Burnham Road from 1941 to 1969.
33 Sink and disposal stoppages
15 toilet stoppages
10 Dishwasher repairs
15 Bath and Basin stoppages.
Pencils, pens, combs, keys, silverware, clothing,

buckles, marbles, etc. recovered were never counted up.

Sometime in the forties our man, Steve Mullin, went to your house for a waste problem. When he arrived, he found you had attempted to fix the problem at the sink with a Stilson wrench. Steve promptly went to the basement to open the drain. On departure he said to you: "Mr. De Haven, you announce on the radio, and I'll do the plumbing."

You had a big water heater connected to the master bath and one to the children's bath. When they ran out of hot water, that was their problem. Did you ever tell them why you were so calm about it all?"

Sincerely,
D.C. Flatten - Bob - Roger - Skip.

The Burnham Road Gang in 1950. The three girls are Helen, Heidi and Molly long before they graduated from the University of Wisconsin. Big Daddy De Haven is looking at mother. John, four years old then, sits on the floor.

Chapter Eleven

There's one advantage to being poor — a doctor will cure you faster.
—*Kin Hubbard, Abe Martin's Sayings, 1915.*

AS NATURALLY AS FARMING comes to a farmer's son and selling to a salesman's son, speaking in public came naturally to me. My father was a facile ad lib speaker, adept at making events flow when he acted as master of ceremonies, a fancy term that came much later. He joined the Four Minute Men during War I, a group of volunteers, named for the Minute Men of the American Revolution. The speakers were limited to four minutes (please note well you present day speakers) in making their appeals for the sales of Liberty Bonds to support the war.

Eleven years old in 1919, I prepared, as a school assignment, my own selling speech for Liberty Bonds. The high point of my talk was my use of the word 'tintinabulation', wow, in the phrase, "the tintinabulation of the bells will herald victory for the Allies." (You can look it up.) The speech I tried out on my family, and my father commented thusly: "That's all right for a talk, Sonny, just don't go too fast; now you can take my place at the Auditorium tomorrow night." The Auditorium was a movie house on Michigan Street, very familiar to me, and I experienced no trepidation or worry about the sudden assignment. Sometimes ignoring a danger is mistaken for courage.

The following night we went to the Auditorium and stood backstage until the end of the silent movie and a few chords of attention from the live pianist in the pit. The house lights came up. "Go on out," John ordered. No wringing of the hands, no frantic good luck wishes, no balconey. My dad treated me as an equal, ignoring the possibility I might be unsure or even frightened. Before I reached center stage, a voice from the front row, which I recognized as belonging to a school chum, one Bill Myers, reassured me. "Give 'em hell, Bob."

I delivered the speech, well under four minutes, and the awakened bells have been tintinabulating ever since.

My dad taught me Lesson One in appearing before an audience: Do it. Just do it. As fundamental as that. Thanks to him, I have had success in speaking and master of ceremonying, and I have been a tiny voice in the homefront office of four wars and in the success of citizens trying to be good citizens.

The natural suspicion of "The Speaker of the Evening" is understandable to me. He has come to educate, harangue, super-sell; some authority has granted him permission to confront the guiltless members of the audience and change their minds about something. An easy manner that creates comfort and confidence in those out front blunts this stiff, sometimes hostile, reception. (A professional speech teacher could tear this advice to bits too small for the shredder.) You don't act the role of "The Speaker;" you become one of the audience who talks. This is easy to do.

I recall two openings to two appearances of my own. Nothing terrific, but they are perfect illustrations of my advice. Way back, parking meters were installed and operative in downtown Minneapolis streets on a Monday. On Thursday, I was handling some kind of a public luncheon at which Judge Levi Hall was the speaker. I introduced him with a line such as, "Excuse Judge Hall if he seems in a hurry. He must get back to City Hall before one-thirty to put a nickel in the meter." I cite this to show the easy way to amuse an audience, not with "clap hands, here I am, the gift to entertainment," but with an obvsious topical remark that involves the speaker, his listeners and a new wrinkle in city living.

(I think of the genius of characterization in the Helen Hokinson cartoon in the New Yorker of a hefty club woman speaking to her club members, holding papers, and saying, "Before I give my report, remember I said before I took office I never wanted to be Treasurer.")

Phil Pillsbury, then President of the company that carries this family name, entertained a group of employees in a hotel ballroom. Backstage, just before the start of the program, Pillsbury asked me what radio shows I appeared on. This was an understandable procedure because I did shows daily at that time, and he wanted to name them all. He wrote the titles on an envelope. In front of his employees, he alluded to me, then removed the envelope from his coat pocket and named the show titles.

On I came to shake hands with Pillsbury, who departed. I spoke to the crowd, "Thank you for that introduction ..." I looked offstage. "Thank you ... Mr. AH ... a." I pulled an envelope from my coat pocket, looked at it and finished the sentence, "Mr. Phillip Pillsbury." The laughter was loud and spontaneous. Any working stiff enjoys a rib of his boss. While not every stiff can or will do this himself, he enjoys an outsider talking back, but gently, to Mr. Big.

My style, if I have a style, excludes harsh words, profanity, smirking allusions to toilets, manure, centerfolds, sex acts and sex deviates. Material such as that produces some laughs, and some of the laughs produced are those of embarrassment of offended people. One entertains by offending? Anyone can write his name on an outhouse wall — anyone. But that doth not a comedian make. The broken limits of property, broken in those lovely sixties, should be restored. A woman can be free and still treated by tenderness and respect. I cringe for ladies and for myself when comedy takes over the human body as its domain. Gynecology is a medical discipline, necessary and most unfunny; leave it that way.

When criticized for off-color material and subjects, some performers will plead that the public is now ready for this treatment or they say, "We give them what they want." Okay, Mr. Big-in-charge-of-programs, you are talking about garbage while sniggering your self-serving alibis for ignoring the needs of youngsters and decent people. I hope you are all successful, save your money and invest in larger and larger supplies of "what people want" — maybe — narcotics.

The accomplished master of ceremonies is an operative in a delicate procedure — the guiding of an entertainment or a ceremony or an after-dinner program. He acts as stage manager, announcer and advisor to those who have planned and planned; he works deftly behind and before the scenes to make the job come off in proper time and with proper consideration of all feelings involved.

The emcee lives by brevity, good humor, consideration of others. He has the ability to bring into play a quote, a news item, a piece of business quickly understood by those out front. People go with you when you romp in play that they understand; they love to be entertained; they hope you can entertain — in their language.

The "Man On The Street" broadcast originated in Chicago; we copied it quickly in 1935 in St. Paul and Minneapolis. We interviewed passersby on a busy street corner and found that listeners enjoyed other people. Any person could speak up, and we announcers learned in a hurry how to encourage the interesting talker and to truncate the dull without seeming to do so.

I think of Bill, a reputable nightclub bouncer of enormous physical dimensions. We used to meet on the streets and in the saloons. Bill slapped people on the back, instantly obtaining their undivided attention. On this occasion, Bill shouted to his buddies, "Here's the guy that caused my divorce." I was as curious as were his older friends there about how I had accomplished this split — a split Bill didn't seem to regret at all. Bill lived with his wife in an apartment building; she worked nine-to-five p.m. while Bill worked nine p.m.-to-three a.m. Mornings he slept — or, as he admitted boyishly, except when he visited a lady upstairs. He emerged at the inner rim of our circles of a "man on the street" broadcast at Witt's Market on Hennepin Avenue. I called to him and we chatted on the air. Next day his wife, following her suspicions about her mate's morning habits, challenged him.

"Home yesterday morning?"

"Of course, I was home. Honest to God."

"All morning?"

"Like I said."

She then fired her salvo, "Then who was that 'Bill' on the radio from Hennepin Avenue? I can't believe a word you say."

The divorce, made not in heaven but on the radio, followed.

The "audience participation" method worked then, now and in between. For six or seven years I traveled every Saturday to a different hardware store of a chain that served Minnesota and three other states. Small town and country people came to see the show, hear the western music, see me and go on the air if they wished. Not much of a program on paper. Listeners and visitors loved the thing.

One day I stumbled on a line that I used several times afterward. In speaking on the mike to a very happy and unpretty farm woman, I asked how many children she had. "I have eleven," she said. This could have gone for a few titters or a laugh, but I stopped that by saying, "Wonderful! Where there's room in the heart, there's room in the house." Surely I am the only person who remembers that remark, but the few words did put this fat lady at ease and paid her a deserved compliment.

Welcome a person's own joke about his own name; don't you joke about his name. An announcer of experience and feeling will, when possible, determine in advance the pronunciation of a name coming up. When unprepared, simply ask, "How do you pronounce your name?" Should he answer, "Adrian Mucklefuss, The Third," repeat his pronunciation precisely with no giggle added. His name is his precious possession; you ought to show respect for it. (You might have answered, "The Third, eh. I didn't know you played in the infield," and with that drawn a few laughs and one hurt. Don't.)

As emcee of carefully produced shows and on those thrown together carelessly, I have played some amusing scenes. In Red Wing, Minnesota, a friend of mine was dedicating his new grain elevator. On a Mississippi river shore at the scene of the ceremony, a small stage had been built of two-by-fours, decorated by flags and bunting and the ribbon to be cut. The man in charge, right-hand man of my friend, dashed about handling last second details; right-hand men are usually harried, and, in this case, he was happy to see me show up and to see the U.S. Congressman from the First District, August Andresen, the ribbon cutter.

His Honor and I were standing on the stage, talking about nothing, when the right-hand man rushed past, calling, "The scissors. WHERE ARE THEY? The scissors for the ribbon cutting?"

Andresen, the paragon of dignity and calm, answered the call, "Wait." In the stern authority of a Shogun declaring war or a Washington crossing the Delaware, he drew from an inside pocket a ten-inch pair of scissors. "I have them here," he said, "My own." Quickly to me, under his voice, the Congressman revealed, "They always forget the scissors."

Live and personal contact creates the ultimate in communication, exceeding the effect of radio and television. A cartoon in the forties in the heyday of Eleanor Roosevelt's crisscrossing America and globe-trotting the world illustrates my point. The drawing shows the low entrance of a straw hut in Africa where the lady of the house is dumping vegetables into a stew pot over a wood fire. Onto this scene has come her husband, pulling a small cart. "What did you do in town?" she asks. "Oh, I sold the cabbage and melons right away, stopped for a beer, shook hands with Mrs. Roosevelt and came home."

Radio's "fame" made me an attraction for public events and small affairs down to the sewing club in the church basement. Adjusting to the exact needs of a committee running a show (and how they appreciate a professional touch) is easy. More importantly, I felt a strong obligation to help in community affairs. My customers were the radio followers; when they needed a favor, I tried to respond. My wife ended a grumbling episode of mine one day when I was feeling put upon by requests for free jobs. Quietly she advised, "Those who can, should." A woman of few words.

Father Tom Meagher, a Roman Catholic priest, has gone to his reward which can only be munificent. He labored for Catholic Charities most of his life. We'd meet at luncheons and dinners where he was usually the clergyman to speak the invocation which he did with dispatch. I complimented him one noon on his speed, just before the start of a luncheon. His only reply: "I use only twelve seconds." I timed him. Eleven seconds.

Father Tom asked me to act as Santa Claus for a group at a Catholic orphanage. In my suit and with distended belly, whiskers and all, I stood waiting for the kids. As they entered I said to Father Tom, "Beautiful kids." He was not so sentimental. He answered: "They don't all need to be here, except for their sonsabitchin' parents."

For about twenty years, a feature of the Minneapolis Aquatennial, a summer funfest, consisted of a luncheon for the state's mayors and spouses. I handled this as emcee, always sitting next to Muriel Humphrey, Mrs. Hubert.

Public relations people who work for charitable agencies needing a free emcee now and then are capable people-handling people. For fun, I recall one experience, not to complain.

Call her Milly. She worked for the St. Paul Community Chest and called to ask me to emcee a report luncheon of the fund solicitors. Our dialog is clear in my memory.

"Oh, Bob, we just needed someone to pep-up the meeting of the various teams. We need you to make it interesting — pizzazzie. At the St. Paul Athletic Club — take about an hour, and no one can do this like you." I said yes.

Second year: "Bob, this is Milly at the Chest. Remember me — Milly? You were such a hit a year ago at our report luncheon everybody wants you back again ... will you come?" She said more and I said yes. Note how Milly is building me up.

Third year: "Bob this is old Milly, how are you? Report Luncheon in two weeks. Can we count on you, Bob dear?"

"Milly, I've done this two years in a row ... isn't there somebody ...?"

"But, Bob, NOW you are a tradition!"

"Okay, I'll come." What else could a tradition have said?

When I was about nine years old, my Uncle Tom Davis backed out his Apperson-Jackrabbit from the barn and we tooled the thirty miles to the Indiana State Fair at Indianapolis. This spectacle of good people, gathered after the harvest, sealed my affection for farmers, small-towners and their families. In 1934, my station in Minneapolis, WTCN, spent a week broadcasting from the Minnesota State Fair. We could outdo our competition in public events and sports because we had no network to steal our good time. I worked following fairs for the next thirty-four years, missing one or two possibly, shaking hands, greeting strangers, broadcasting on radio and talking on public address mikes. Meeting those they hear on the air is still a treat for those in the crowds. We handed out no souvenirs, pictures, perhaps, and when at WCCO, we did feature ice water. I'd kid the management gently by inviting them to "Come on ovah, hurry, hurry, hurry! See the real, live people who broadcast to you every day. Joyce Lamont, down from Duluth for the last time in the twentieth century — the great Cedric Adams in his high school graduation suit — Boone and Erickson, the single act that looks like two people. And to top off this munificent display of bountifulness, we'll let you serve yourself a free paper cup of guaranteed ice water, courtesy of big-hearted 'CCO."

After one of those myriad appearances, I walked down a street toward my car, and a fellow, blue-shirted, brown jacket, came along side me. "Hi, Bob," he said. We talked.

"I'm from Spring Valley, Wisconsin," he announced. "'Bout sixty miles away. Gee, that's a wonderful place. Been in St. Paul two days, and I'm anxious to go home. You'd like Spring Valley, Bob."

That's America. My eyes filled up, but he could not see that reaction. We shook hands, and he wandered away. A few days afterward, I opened a letter from this man. There was only his name on the back of a snapshot of the main street of Spring Valley, Wisconsin. "God shed his grace on thee."

In rummaging for a notation for this book (couldn't find it), I came onto pages marked "Personal Appearances." They were part of a longer list, pages of which are missing. What I found starts with October 8, 1944, and the second sheet ends on the date, November 28, 1944. The total of appearances is thirty-six. Naming a few will suggest the variety of the gatherings: Minnesota Editorial Association, talk; Tom Dewey Rally, master of ceremonies; Veterans Hospital, pheasant dinner; Navy Day Rally, University of Minnesota; Adath Jushurun Synagogue, war bond rally; Fort Snelling Officers' Wives Club; Incarnation Church, Santa Claus; Women's Club, drama section; Fort Snelling Field House, bond rally; Minneapolis Star-Tribune carriers, talk. I've done graduation addresses, one of these before St. Barnabas Hospital nurses from the pulpit of an Episcopal Cathedral.

For two campaigns of the Minneapolis United Way I acted as Chairman of the speakers' bureau; therefore, I was pleased to see my own total of speeches made during the second campaign. Thirty-one. I was sure I was champ. Then came a sheet for Don Stoltz, owner of The Old Log Theater, Excelsior, Minnesota — fifty-three. Sit down, De Haven!

*　　*　　*

Along came Dr. George Young.

This character contributed flashes of his flamboyant character to early broadcasting in the Twin Cities. Fate started him in the broadcasting business, and he did the rest. Doc had ordered some equipment for his optical business located in a Northside storefront, where he fitted glasses and sold his wares. The heavy freight shipment arrived containing nothing he had ordered. The contents baffled his power to identify it; so he called in an engineer. The person declared the machinery a broadcast transmitter. Doc never returned the transmitter. He became a broadcaster.

Always running third or fourth best, after the business grew a little, Doc didn't mind; he thrashed around on and off the air, drove fancy cars and flew an airplane. His presence was anything but a secret. The station call letters were chosen from the acronym of his initials — WDGY. He should have written a book.

But Doc sold out for good money along in the Fifties. In the Sixties, Young America switched its culture and WDGY fed the music these people worshipped — rock and roll. WDGY's announcers became screamers to the delight of all except those who tire of visiting a zoo and those others involved in broadcasting in the same town. We standard bearers at the dominant WCCO were sure of our position until 'DGY came along to challenge our ramparts.

The 'DGY management started to give away cash; listeners tuned in to test the giveaway. A short, simple phrase would be repeated in a time segment on the air; other phrases followed in later segments. A cash sum, ranging from fifty to one-thousand dollars, was offered the listener who knew the phrase (by listening, of course) and, if telephoned by the announcer, could repeat the phrase to him. This gimmick brought listeners and set off a hullabaloo of publicity.

WCCO stroked its beard, glanced at its high ratings and decided to go with exactly the same format by throwing cash around, which action created a standoff. The tie was broken when 'DGY announced, "We've been told that the high and mighty WCCO has started to give away cash, as we have been doing for two weeks. BUT, we have a plan to protect you from missing any of our wonderful music. We will broadcast the WCCO clues here on WDGY, along with ours, so you listen only to our station to get the clues for *both* contests.

For ten years I had been doing the 7:15 a.m. newscast, prime time with prime ratings. On one Thursday morning, our newswriters, headed by Chuck Sarjeant, were slipping the last pages into place about 7:10 a.m. Sarjeant's wife telephoned to notify us of the new twist, just announced on 'DGY, of arrogance in this contest of wits and popularity. The pilfering of our clues! GEE!

In a pique that would have done a department of state proud, we gabbed about the possibilities of a counter move. This was truly war; I went into the announcer's booth with my news copy, our innocuous clue for our giveaway and no plan to thwart the opposition.

A flirty and devious little angel who sits on my shoulder started to whisper, accompanied in the background by two harps. She called for yet another switch. When I came to the spot of our giveaway, I adlibbed the "winning phrase," which 'DGY had promised to repeat for their listeners: "Day in and day out, you hear the most dependable radio news on good old WCCO."

Surprise! WDGY announcer must have careened into shock. Their man aired the WCCO promotion blurb on their station immediately and continued to put ours on their air that night, through Friday and Saturday. Sunday afternoon it stopped. Our fun ended, also; part of that fun was composing new 'CCO blurbs for their listeners.

A week or so later, both stations realized the scheme was costly and that it was tiring out. Both dropped the giveaway. WCCO had turned back the Rebs at Cemetery Ridge.

Chapter Twelve

The only way a problem can be solved is to find an answer
to it.

—*Ben Berger*

BEFORE ME LIES a book entitled, *How To Break Into Radio*, published by Harper & Brothers, New York and London, 1941. On the flyleaf in my handwriting: "At some time or other all people born in Indiana write a book. According to the public radio, I qualify as being born in Indiana, and, as I am quite busy in a radio career (?), I thought I would get this book writing out of the way. I broke into radio without a book but not without the loving patience of Mom and Pop. This is your copy from one of the authors: Bob. March 18, 1941."

My partner, Harold S. Kahm, is credited on the title page with authoring *New Business Opportunities For Today* and *How to Make The Most Of Your Life*. Harold's proposition to me was simple: "You know how a person makes it into radio; I know how to sell a book. Let's work together." I wrote the "how to"; he sold the tome. My byline is decorated with "Production Manager and Program Director, Station WTCN, Minneapolis-St. Paul."

Now the volume serves well my backward look at broadcasting. The tender thing is a perfectly preserved excavation of a record, in modern English, of the business at the turn to the Forties.

The book starts with two surprising lines: "Along with fabulous Hollywood the radio industry pays the highest average salaries in the world. This statement is based on wage tabulations and estimates compiled by the Federal Government." A tempting lure for the ambitious.

Among the thirteen chapters are these: "How to Obtain Radio Experience," "So You Want to Be An Annoucer?" "Television and Your Future."

Television and your future? Look at what this upstart wrote forty-four years ago: "It's only a question of time before nearly every home in the United States will be equipped with a television theater. These television sets will probably have screens, not merely a few inches in size, but rather several feet; perhaps the television screen of the future may occupy half the wall of the average living room. These units will offer on a big scale what is now given to the public in a limited way, namely the telecasting of public sporting events, dramatic plays and other entertainment."

Not an inconsequential prediction in 1941 for a working stiff with no time to look into a crystal ball, if he had access to one. Quoting here from my earlier "work" might damage sales of "How To Break ..." that have been humming along at zero since publication. But that's the book business which is another subject for another book.

To the hopeful and ambitious I did recommend sternly, the values of education in high school, radio school or college; I hammered on the necessity of understanding events in the news, the community affairs where you live, the way the advertising game is played, the elements of a simple sentence, vocabulary and the intelligent use of The King's English.

Was there opportunity in 1941? Sure there was. I listed in the book the radio stations in America, and they numbered 750. Truly an infant industry. Now there are approximately 9512. Baby, look at you now.

"One item from my "Glossary of Radio Slang and Expression" will suffice. "On the nose — An Expression meaning a program's timing is working out exactly right, when it is neither ahead of the rehearsed time nor behind it." (As the nose itself which is only a nose, if it is neither too far ahead or too far behind the face.)

The final chapter of this early opus (a word Clelland Card wryly pronounced oh, puss, as in Benny Goodman's "Oh, Puss ½") still carries sums of interest, lore for oldsters who remember the broadcasters of another day and a gleam of hope for beginners. To furnish my last chapter of "How to Break ..." with experiences of others, I wrote to performers then on the air to ask each for the story of how he got his start. These people walk on here from the past with their lines written to me. My introduction in the book: "The opportunities are just as numerous today as they ever were, and the methods for breaking in are just as varied, for radio is still in its infancy."

Don MacNeill, Master of Ceremonies, Breakfast Club, NBC, Chicago. "I got acquainted with the Chief Announcer of Station WISN, Milwaukee, while attending Marquette University. I started part-time announced at same station while in college and gradually worked into acting on programs as a master of ceremonies."

Trafton Robertson, Announcer, WBT, Charlotte, North Carolina. "One sunny Virginia day while strolling down one of Norfolk's verdant fairways with two companions, we were moved to song, perhaps in an effort to forget the bad golf. We were good, and further investigation revealed that we were the male Boswell Sisters. Getting on the air was only a matter of auditioning at the local station, WTAR. Making money was more difficult. We dissolved. I formed another group and got on again. One night the announcer for our program didn't show up, and I shyly volunteered to take his place. All this in '31. The station manager heard me announce. When a staff man resigned, the boss' secretary suggested I audition, and I did. I got the job, got fired, got rehired. I have been announcing and singing ever since. It's good work, and I got it through the ambitions of a trio of singing golfers. I thank you." (Robertson now lives in Norfolk, Virginia.)

Kate Smith, Singing Star, CBS, New York. "Before getting into radio I had been in vaudeville since I was eleven years old. After appearing on Broadway in *Flying High*, I decided to quit show business and become a nurse. But Ted Collins, then an executive of a recording company, heard me and asked me to make some recordings for him. After this he became my manager. A few months later he got me a job doing sustaining programs on CBS. Before long I had my own commercial."

Bob Heiss, Chief Announcer, WTMJ, Milwaukee, Wisconsin. "I was a prize. Seven years back, the depression had sent me into dance music. I was a saxaphone player and a crooner ... with some ambitions of being a radio announcer simply because several people with whom I had numerous phone conversations frequently remarked that I had announcer qualifications. WTMJ's management didn't feel that way, however. But one day someone hit upon the idea, as a publicity gag, of opening auditions to the general public. One of the authors (guess who) of this book was announcing a pickup of our band at the Vanity Cafe, and I asked him if the contest was on the level. He assured me it was. My application was among the eight hundred that were received. Over four hundred auditions were given. Thirty-four second auditions were given. Four were chosen for further consideration. Finally they pointed to one man. And here I am."

Graham McNamee, Announcer, NBC, New York. "It was a mild curiosity and lack of anything else to do that led me to visit the old WEAF studios in the AT&T Building on lower Broadway that eventful day in May, 1923. I was a concert singer serving on jury duty at the time, and we were released early that day. The weather was fine and I decided to walk down to the Battery. What made me walk down the West side of Broadway instead of the East side I don't know, but I crossed the street and began walking.

"As I strolled, my thoughts were on the concert season just concluded, the engagements and the favorable comment my baritone voice had aroused in the press. I had debuted in Aeolian Hall in 1921 and fairly well established in my career, but I wondered what I would do until the next season began in October.

"I came out of my reverie was I approached the AT&T Building at 195 Broadway and recalled that a friend had told me about a radio station being opened there just a few days before. On an impulse I went in and asked to see them. Someone directed me to Sam Ross, then and still a talent scout for NBC. Ross was proud of the new layout and took me around. We grew quite friendly, and he began asking questions about me. I told him of my concert work and the jury duty and my thoughts of a moment before.

"Ross asked me to sing before the microphone and then to speak into it. I obliged and it turned into an audition. For the speaking lines I discussed recent events in the sports world and when I got through Ross pegged me as a cross between a singer and a sports expert and offered me a job.

"Well, I stipulated I would take the job of announcer until the concert season opened in October. We also agreed that I was to do little or no singing. Professional reasons dictated that reservation.

"We covered several big outdoor events that season, among them an all-important world's heavyweight championship fight, and my fate was sealed. Radio and its possibilities got into my blood, and I couldn't quit when October came around. But I didn't drop my concert work. I somehow managed to get in both although radio was taking up more and more of my time.

"In 1927, '28 and '29 I filled more than a hundred concernt dates per year. It wasn't until 1930 that I was forced to give it up entirely, due to the pressure of radio activities."

Blaine Cornwell, Program Director, KXOK, St. Louis, Missouri. "I was the baritone soloist at Saint Thomas Church in Washington, D.C., and one of the men in the bass section had done some announcing in Washington and Baltimore. He urged me to take an audition for announcing, but I thought then that radio was not here to stay. Most of my living I earned working in the bookkeeping department of a bank. Home one day with a cold, my singer-friend called me to tip me off about an opening at WRC. He was so insistent that I audition, he wouldn't take "no" for an answer. I auditioned and went to work for NBC five days later."

Ray Kelly, Manager Sound-Effects Development, NBC,

New York. "I didn't exactly break into radio. I was a victim of circumstances. When I took the job in February, 1930, I was doing quite well out in Seminole, Oklahoma as the District Clerk for the Seminole products area of the Gypsy Oil Company. Even the title is impressive.

"Ignorant of the fate that awaited me, I began training for the job of inventing noises and sounds for radio while a student at Knox College, Galesburg, Illinois. There I met C.L. Menser, who ran the Speech Department and directed and staged theatricals for the Knox College Players Club, the student dramatic society.

"Not realizing what I was getting into, I found myself drafted for the job of constructing the scenery and arranging the sets for Menser's masterpieces. After graduation, believing all that was past, I entered Harvard Law School. I was getting along nicely until a year-and-a-half later — the crash of 1929.

"Well, Menser and I kept up an intermittent correspondence during this period and in the interim he had landed a job with the National Broadcasting Company as a production director in New York. Always a bug for realism, he discovered a void in radio drama. Sound effects were deemed to aid the listener in creating a visual setting for the drama.

"For him, to think is to act and the next thing I knew I received a letter proclaiming the dire need of my services and was so moved by his appeal. I took the next train east. And here I am, a grown man, making gadgets that squeak for the microphone. It's interesting, if slightly unbalanced, however, and I'm very fond of the work.

Agnes Moorhead, Actress, NBC, New York. "I entered radio during a moment of indecision. A graduate of the American Academy of Dramatic Art with some radio experience gained as the girl baritone on KMOX and KSD, St. Louis, plus parts in broadway shows, were my only assets when I tried out for radio dramatics.

"However, the story goes back a bit. While a student at the Academy, one of my instructors was Joseph Bell, who is now Production Director for the National Broadcasting Company.

Upon leaving the Academy, I obtained parts in several broadway shows. After nearly a year knocking about the stage, I was offered a role in the show *Candlelight*. It was while trying to make up my mind whether to accept a part that might take me away from other possible offers that the die was cast. My story proves that you never know how it will happen in radio.

"I happened to meet Mr. Bell one day. He had like my work at the Academy and gave me every encouragement. He had left school shortly after I did to go with NBC. When I told him of my unsettled situation, he suggested I come up to NBC with him and audition for a dramatic role that was open. I got the part and here I am.

"My previous radio experience had been as a member of the St. Louis Municipal Opera Company, with which I had earned the questionable distinction of singing baritone parts. The local stations mentioned above engaged me as a singer and billed me as the "Baritone Girl." It was dreadful, though interesting, and after a short time I quit to go to college and then to the Academy.

Bily Rhoades, Junior, Sports Annoucer, WSAU, Wausau, Wisconsin. "I first broke into radio September first, 1936, at Grand Forks, North Dakota. Previously, my only experience in radio had been gained through a few dramatic shows and covering high school events for a special school-news program on WTCN in the Twin Cities. I got the Grand Forks job by auditioning with several others. I worked there until I was let out at the end of six months. I took to the road via my thumb and auditioned at several Wisconsin stations. I have held two since then and before coming to WSAU. Fortunately I have never been afraid to ask for a job or ask for a ride on the road. Over one weekend I hopped to Omaha to try for a sports announcing job, which I didn't get. But you've got to keep trying. I have averaged a job for every six auditions, which may not prove anything at all statistically.

"And, furthermore, I hope I don't have to change jobs so often now that I'm specializing and getting some sound experience."

And so much for my first book effort. I write a book every

forty-four years; so save your money for the next publication in 2029.

*   *   *

Along came Ken Downs.

Ken journeyed to Chicago by freight car from his hometown somewhere in Montana and thence to Milwaukee to look for a job. He caught on as a reporter at Hearst's Wisconsin News. Downs was five feet something, brown mustache, wiry, strong, polite and tough. He and I were inhabitants, with four other newspaper and radio guys, in the penthouse of the Royal Hotel, a block from the best hotel in town, the Schroeder. Well, we were close to the best anyway.

The furnished penthouse (mostly in reds) offered five bedrooms, three baths, dining room, living room, telephone nook and a reputation which would rate somewhere below "fair minus." A weighty steel door with peephole permitted entrance after a visitor walked up one flight from the last elevator stop. A former gambling joint? Yes, a gambling joint until we moved in, engaging Joe Budar, manager, in a gamble for his rent. With maid service yet, we paid six dollars each per week. This piece of a hotel in the radiant year of 1931 became a terminus of the underground railway carrying newsmen and radio announcers looking for work. The worldly needs of these itinerants were covered by our charity and mental mumblings of "I may be the next one who needs a place to sleep." We discovered freedom; rather Freedom long before the denizens of Haight-Ashbury in San Francisco, although I don't remember any of us handing out flowers to strangers.

The door with the peephole was always unlocked. I filed in my memory two successive nights because of the difference in the quality of guests that were entertained. Monday — the girls from the Empress Burlesque Theater. Tuesday — the girls from the Ziegfeld Follies playing the Davidson Theater.

I didn't pay much attention, if you can believe that, because I needed to arise early and go to work.

Ken Downs talked softly and revealed by action his love of

— 162 —

fearless adventure. There were two brothers, call them Dick and Mike, from Manitowoc, Wisconsin, who succeeded in several highjackings in Milwaukee. In fleeing from the law officers, they became separated. Downs wheedled a tip from one of the girl friends about the location of Mike. Downs found him, drunk, in an apartment near downtown. In the course of an hour's chat, while the felon remained in bed, Downs convinced him that his brother awaited him at the Wisconsin News office. Downs offered to take him there, an offer that made sense to the boozy crook because the brothers needed to put their stories and alibis straight. Before Mike would leave the apartment, he tried to obtain a wallet from a dresser drawer. Downs talked him out of that desire but got a peek in the drawer, finding only a .45, which Downs appropriated.

At the city room of the News, Mike met, not his brother, but Herman Ewald, City Editor, who was smaller than Downs, and an assortment of police officers. The quiet Downs had a scoop. I asked him, "What did Mike do when he saw the cops?"

"He gave me a dirty look that made me glad there was a cop on either side of him."

Another brother act in Wisconsin crime history was engaged in by huskies we'll call Bill and Joe. They were farm boys who tired of the hours required and the lack of a future. They took off to seek success in knocking over a Wisconsin bank, and, finding this easy to do, launched a crime spree, traveling the state and taking along the lover of one brother, a teenaged female named Minnie Pliska. Her age added kidnapping to the bank robbery charge. The profitable business expanded to Minnesota and the two Dakotas with the cops always one bank behind. Of course, these depredations and the girl made sensational newspaper headlines.

Then ... Minnie disappeared from the team. Where was Minnie, the headlines demanded? Well, I bumped into the girl one afternoon about two when I came home from work at WTMJ, the Milwaukee Journal station and found the iron door of the penthouse chained shut. My emotions churned with fury at this lockout from my own hotel suite. My screams and pounding on the door brought a steely eye to the peephole; then the door opened and Downs explained calmly, "Oh, I thought you were the cops." Minnie's voice tinkled from the living room.

Indeed, the police and other reporters were searching frantically for Miss Pliska, whom Downs, by some means of guile or abuse of the truth had located and taken into his own custody. For four days they had hidden out in an apartment, other than the penthouse of The Royal. Maybe the afternoon I ran into them they were slumming.

The clever Downs, who mixed his chivalry with his profession, was writing installments of her life story — Minnie Pliska's journey as a gun moll. This was stuff of sensation, exclusive for the Wisconsin News, and stuff that infuriated police and the august Milwaukee Journal. Downs faced trouble, but not until he was caught and until he squeezed everything Herman Ewald wanted in the Pliska life story. His final installment ended with a single-sentence paragraph. "Minnie Pliska was found this morning on the main floor of a building at 333 North State Street," the address of the Milwaukee Journal. And that was correct. Downs must have grinned through his brown mustache when he notified the police, on a Milwaukee Journal telephone, to look in the lobby of the building of his opposition paper.

My small part in the scoop came the next day when Walter (The Great You-Know-What) Damm called me in. He was not smiling.

"You live in a hotel with this Downs?"

"Yes."

"Downs will get a jail term, you know, for obstructing justice. She's a bank robber. Harry Grant is mad as hell at the news." (Grant was only the mighty publisher of the mighty Journal.) "Now I'm not the one to tell anybody where to live, but, when Harry Grant asks me if you live in the Royal, I'd better, for you sake, answer 'No'. Do you know what I mean?"

"I think I do, Mr. Damm."

That night, that very same night, the future Dennis Morgan of Warner Brothers, borrowed his father's car to pick me up with my worldly possessions, which fit nicely into the Hupmobile roadster, and moved me from the penthouse to the Tower Hotel, kitty corner from Marquette University.

The robbing brothers were captured, Downs escaped without charge, much less conviction; Minnie went on to better days; all was right with the world.

Chapter Thirteen

Many times I have been introduced to an audience as 'Dr. Charles Mayo, son of the famous Mayo brothers,' and that is a biologic impossibility.

—*Dr. Charlie Mayo*

THERE WAS A TIME, my children, when there were no word processors, margination and page framers and other such aids to transferring material from the heads of writers to the printed pages. Classified Ad sections of newspapers could not be remade up by a flick of an electronic key; so late-arriving items were squeezed in under a heading that read: TOO LATE TO CLASSIFY, which phrase describes this chapter. Here are items demanding only a moment from a reader. In gathering scraps of paper to write a book, some seem to slip to the floor and pile up in distant corners. Some of these I have rescued in order to preserve them here for the ages ...

*   *   *

One of Chicago's best hotels around the middle of the century was the Blackstone on Michigan Avenue. My wife and I managed to afford a room there one night. In the lobby, I recognized Alexander Woollcott, writer, critic, even actor, who was hitting the top doing network radio. Breaking my own rule about encroaching on celebrities, I introduced myself, saying I liked his stuff and that I was from Minnesota. Quickly he quipped, "Minnesota and Duluth, zenith city of the unsalted sea."

*　　*　　*

Why hasn't some wag used the obvious phrase, "Between IRAQ and a hard place?"

*　　*　　*

The Afternoon Show served as title for an hour-long variety program I emceed daily on WTMJ. This was filled with a big band, singers, whistlers, instrumentalists and other variety acts. Pay for these — three bucks a show. We did well. On Thursdays, a proud father, who looked and acted Italian, brought his son, Walter, to play the piano. The kid was too young to come downtown alone, but he was surprisingly accomplished on his instrument and surprisingly accomplished at maintaining a broad smile for everyone who looked at him. The smile was natural because it never quit; nor did Walter lose his ingratiating manner. In time, he did drop one thing — his first name. This left only — Liberace.

*　　*　　*

The Dispatch Was There! I thought that an attractive title for a newspaper promotion show on radio. For one of WTCN's owners we put together a weekly series on momentous and historical regional stories of the past. You may recall a program called *CBS Was There.* You recall with accuracy, but the network conjured up the ideas years after I had done my conjuring. Our angle, which was effective promotional advertising, pointed out the importance of the newspaper's coverage and how this coverage was obtained. Inside stuff on a background of history. Where possible, we quoted the newspaper people who worked the story.

We dramatized the Sioux Indian Uprising in Minnesota;

the purloining of the official copy of a new state statute that would have moved the capitol from St. Paul to St. Peter; a gun fight between a militant farmer and officers of the State of Wisconsin over a dam on his property; and the Hinckley forest fire. That disaster took over 400 lives and devastated an entire county in North Central Minnesota. One group of terrified people escaped on a locomotive that steamed out of the fire from the town of Hinckley. I placed in my dramatization an imagined couple, trapped in a well they had entered for safety but were immediately threatened there by death from smoke suffocation. In a few spoken words they admitted the end was near. Praying in unison, they started The Lord's Prayer. One voice trailed off; before the end of the familiar words the other voice coughed three times and then ceased, leaving only silence. Pretty good dramatic stuff.

Another such writing effort I appropriately called *The Hanging of Harry Hayward*.

In the early '90's, Harry played well the role of a foppish man-about-town, Minneapolis. His penchant for girls and dislike for work programmed him for trouble. He caught up with an attractive female, Kitty Ging, a new seamstress in town from the East, who, between stitches, searched for a better opportunity. She and he started to keep company. He bought an insurance policy on her life. For a modern reader or TV viewer, this ploy would be a dead giveaway of Harry. He hired a heavy drinker, janitor of the Ozark Flats (now Belleview Manor) on Hennepin Avenue named Claus Blixt, to pick up Kitty at the West Hotel, presumably to drive her to a rendez-vous with Hayward. But no — Blixt drove her in the buggy to the West shore of Lake Calhoun, South of downtown, where he earned his fee by bashing in her head and shooting her dead. The horse, as always in tales of those days, returned to the livery stable, pulling an empty buggy.

Hayward was a suspect from the start. His nervous brother, Adry, turned him in. Harry Hayward was convicted and hanged in the old Courthouse, the last person to be executed in Hennepin County. The actual killer and driver of the buggy died in State Prison in 1925.

This story, flowing over the decades with sensational juices, I put into an hour's play, picked a cast and started to rehearse. On Monday, with the broadcast scheduled for Friday, the Minneapolis Tribune started to run full-page ads for "The Harry Hayward Murder." Instantaneous heat appeared, directed at the newspaper and at the radio station. By Wednesday, the cast and the gallows were in place for our production; but the publisher of the paper telephoned to say, "Cancel this thing." I protested — freedom of the press and radio and all that, you know.

His explanation: "There are living relatives of people involved in that murder who will be hurt by such a broadcast." Now, I agree he was right. Recently I looked for the script that died before the Friday, but it has flown away with Kitty Ging and Harry Hayward, denied with them fruition.

* * *

"Senator Capehart (Indiana) is so lucky that, if motherhood was the issue, he would get pregnant." — Irving Liebowitz.

* * *

A priceless gem you may own without rental or purchase: "Here in green meadows sits eternal May." — Robert Herrick, circa 1648.

* * *

If a woman can look deshevelled after a wrestling match, can she look shevelled before?

* * *

For a long time, although not now, a St. Paul family owned and operated a large department store. The President and boss was asked what his younger brother, Harry, did in the store. "Harry? He's in charge of the Toy Department, except at Christmas."

*　　*　　*

Another store, Heller's Furniture Store, in my home town, used a slogan our family repeated and joked about. After more than a half-century, I perceive it to have been an excellent statement of the firm's integrity and, therefore, an excellent advertising slogan. "When Heller says it's oak, it's oak."

*　　*　　*

Walter Reuther led Big Labor into its modern era of power in the country by successfully challenging the auto industry in Detroit. What kind of a person was he? I have one item in the answer. At the University of Minnesota, we staged a broadcast of *Town Meeting* for the Blue Network of NBC. Reuther spoke for labor and the President of a local knitting business spoke for capital. The program's moderator was its well-known founder, George V. Denny of Town Hall, New York.

I asked Reuther for his expense account, which later came in the mail, showing only two items. "Round trip coach fare and one upper berth, $2.50, Detroit to Minneapolis."

*　　*　　*

Eugene Ormandy, former maestro of the Minneapolis Symphony, told this one in an interview on Public TV. "Vienna, Austria, has many places of historical interest that are marked by plaques, stating birth, deaths and stage triumphs of the musically famous. Brahms was walking the town with a music critic named Hanzlich, who pointed to his own flat and asked, 'What sign do you guess will be on that house after I die?' Brahms answered, 'For Rent.'"

*　　*　　*

A fine fellow and friend of mine was Benton Ferguson, advertising and public relations specialist in Minneapolis and Tulsa. On his business stationery this legend was printed:

"Hire me to tell the world how modest you are."

*　　*　　*

Toward a better understanding of the complex world of sport, our author, searching for the only unbiased fan in the sports world, interviews himself.

Q. What kind of a sports fan are you?
A. Avid.
Q. What kinds of sports events do you attend?
A. Crucial and pivotal. All games are crucial and pivotal. I attend the most crucial and most pivotal. I especially enjoy events that inspire slogans such as: "Tough times end; tough people do not," "This is do or die," "There's no tomorrow," and "The team that won't be beat can't be beat," as in synchronized swimming in the Olympic Games.
Q. What do you look for in a football game?
A. A fan, forty-three years old, wearing a parka, climbing an eighth of a mile of concrete steps, carrying seven hot dogs with mustard and catsup, and seven wilting paper cups of coffee and falling down on the top step.
Q. How would you improve parking at the stadium?
A. Reduce the entrance fee to 10¢ and charge a fee of $6 to get out of the lot. In this way the attendants who packed you in would have to wait as long as you to get out. This would draw a new focus on their philosophy of life.
Q. If you occupied your idea of the best seat, where would you be?
A. In the Goodyear blimp. You can see the stadium but not the game, and there is a bar aft.
Q. Are super athletes paid too much money?
A. No, they should be paid more handsomely in order to improve the lot of indigent lawyers and agents who can't make it at these rates.
Q. Do you *really* know any pompom girls?

A. Not really. I winked at one in Dallas on October 23, 1969. She suggested I try The Green-Dappled Retirement Home in Robust, Arkansas. Her uncle owned it.

Q. Why are sports writers so smart on how promoters and owners should spend their money?

A. These fellows have no money of their own, leaving them free to spend all their financial thinking on the monetary problems of others.

Q. Are baseball games too long?

A. Not for me. I never tire of watching a team manager spit and then wipe his chin. That's entertainment.

Q. Is any sport too long?

A. Six-day bike racing in any given six days.

Q. Are baseball statistics valid since parks have different dimensions and some have grass and some artificial turf?

Q. Rubbish. Comiskey Park in Chicago maintains the same dimensions as when it was constructed in 1648. Ask any owner (not a player) about the surfaces. Grass is the same as manufactured turf. (Come to think of it, ask any manufacturer of artificial turf.) On one surface a batted ball strikes the infielder's glove, and on the other the ball strikes the infielder's face between the nose and right eye. What's the difference?

Q. Are concession prices too high?

A. I don't have an opinion. I never buy anything. I ate my last cookie kewpie doll, with a chocolate "P," at West Lafayette, Indiana, in 1927.

Q. Do you listen to the hawkers of concessions?

A. If I can hear them over the radios people carry into the stands. And sometimes the letters on their jackets are more fascinating than the action on the field.

Q. Any opinion on basketball?

A. I enjoy watching the officials. They whistle constantly, but never play a tune. They gesture, indicating a foul, like the prosecutors at the Nuremberg Trials. And I do a great deal of needlepoint during the stalling and called "times-out" near the end.

Q. Did you know Red Smith, the famous sports writer?
A. No, but I wish I had. He was a Notre Dame student when I was enrolled at South Bend High.
Q. Did Red like basketball?
A. I believe not. After Red proposed increasing the basket diameter to six feet and reducing its elevation to three feet, a friend protested, "That would ruin the game." Red answered, "Well ..."
Q. What about tennis?
A. There's something screwy about tennis. Win one point and you get five or fifteen; win two and you have thirty; three and you have forty-five. One more and you don't have fifty; you have one game. If you or your opponent is wiped out, you or he has love. Something like Haigh-Ashbury used to be.

*　　*　　*

Q. What sport is your favorite?
A. "Trivial Pursuit." I invented that one.

*　　*　　*

Saved from "Laugh In," bless its memory.
"Who wants me next door?"
"Everybody in here."
and
"I like working for the National Conference of Christians and Jews. I get 240 holidays a year."

*　　*　　*

A daily grammatical error of announcers who think they are pretty good is illustrated by, "This group is accused of a crime they did not commit."

*　　*　　*

Gay Brewer became a surprise and surprised winner of the Masters Golf Tournament. In the interview after the victory he was asked if he would play in the British Open. "I don't know. When is it?"

*   *   *

Frankie Frisch, way back in radio days, interviewed a winning pitcher after the last game of the World Series in a locker room, storming with macho shouts to the music of free-flowing champagne.

Asked, "Frankie, well, what do you think if it?"

Answered the pitcher, "Of what?"

*   *   *

Calvin Coolidge, when President, honored Northern Wisconsin by taking a week to fish for trout in the Brule River. Howard Joyce, a poker-playing friend of mine, operated a dairy in nearby Ashland and had supplied Coolidge's camp with milk and butter. Joyce told me that he presented a statement for the products at the end of the week, and, in return, he received a personal check for the full amount, signed by Calvin Coolidge himself. The famous Vermonter of the Twenties live out his own creed: "There is no dignity quite so impressive and no independence quite so important as living within your means."

*   *   *

Weather broadcasters, have you ever considered this: "But who wants to be foretold the weather? It is bad enough when it comes with or without our having the misery of knowing about it before hand." — Jerome K. Jerome, *Three Men In A Boat*, 1889.

*   *   *

Sleep with clean hands, either by integrity all day or washed clean at night by repentence." — John Donne.

*   *   *

On the air: "When death breaks up a marriage, the spouse lives longer." Well, I'll be darned.

*   *   *

Fortunately I acquired a jackal's wariness of people who push others around. A bully tries to bluff out his inward fear of a broken nose. I hate 'em. At the other extreme, I happily think of a tribute to Stanley Woodward, sports writer, written upon his death: "Stanley was contemptuous of his superiors, barely tolerant of his equals and unfailingly polite to those beneath him."

*   *   *

My first piece of college copy, a humor column, was pressed on me by a good friend who also wrote for this part of the Op-Ed page of the student newspaper, *The Daily Cardinal*. Writers used nom de plumes. My friend signed Argon The Lazy. Argon is an inert gas. He dubbed me The Half Wit's Half Brother. Naturally, I felt my first effort was petty good: however, the editor to whom I handed the copy perused the sheet solemnly, not a smile. When finished he asked only, "Don't you have any commas on your typewriter?"

As a sometime staffer on *The Daily Cardinal*, I wrote features, or that is what I called them. One subject was "The Indiana Hop" as displayed at a Purdue football dance. Another kidded the Dean of Men for sitting forty-one hours outside an apartment where an unmarried student couple were shacked-up. (Yes, kiddies, such activities existed then — I mean the Dean's.) The two escaped through a window.

I wrote reviews of the vaudeville bills at the Orpheum Theater. Seeing my name in print prompted me to take a journalism course; so I selected "The Writing of Feature Articles," taught by no less than Willard Grosvenor Bleyer, founder of the School of Journalism that became famous at the University of Wisconsin. I recall my sophisticated sniffing at the pages of the textbook, written by Bleyer himself and published seven years before. In his lectures, Bleyer pounded on a point that our article material should be up-to-date, which dictum, in my mind, ruled out a seven-year-old textbook. Oh, I was a finely tuned machine of 19 years of age — confident, critical and dumb.

Wait, Professor Bleyer, or the ghost thereof, I hurry to record here the fact that I did turn into money one of the pieces I wrote for you — 900 words on "How To Turn That Extra Sleeping Room Into Money" for *The Farm Journal* magazine. "Put your best spread on the bed; wash the windows; place a sign on the lawn reading 'Tourist Room'," I advised. My first ever sale of the written word — twenty (20), full-sized, 1927 bucks.

Proving money isn't everything is done easily. For the Haresfoot Club I was called in (later I became a member) to write a musical comedy (the first of three) for the spring tour and I did; the oh puss was entitled *Hi Jack!* Two acts, based on gangland Chicago, music by Jack Mason. We played in it, Jack in the pit — I on the stage, toured to seven cities and made money. My fee and royalty were contained in one check — for fifty dollars.

In the Thirties, a writer could make a start by selling fiction to the pulp magazines, called that because they were printed on cheap pulp paper and sold at ten or fifteen cents an issue. You will see the same pulp story genre on the telly with hoopla and alleged acting stars with the same appeals — excitement and suspense. In that winter of '35 and '36, when the Minneapolis temperature hit 34 below zero in February and did not rise above zero in the twenty-eight days, I arose two hours before time to go to work and, inside a sheepskin overcoat, sat at a typewriter to turn out pulp sport stories. *All America Sports* magazine sent me my first check, ten dollars for "Fielder's Choice." Fine story. The same summer, out of a job, I lolled with my family on the south shore of Lake Superior and eventually sold $750 of my stuff. In 1936 that was a small fortune. My literary betters had chosen garrets on the Left Bank of Gay Parie, but I allow they did not have as much fun as I had.

In trying to write for money, I learned to my amazement, which persists to this day, of the gullibility of readers and listeners. Perhaps gullibility contributes to the charm of human kind; I hope so.

Three examples of this quality come to mind, and they involve Barbara Hutton, Waikiki Beach and my wife, who is known as Hurricane Hat.

The straight humorous piece was once a staple of magazines and newspapers. In columning for the Minneapolis Tribune, I wrote a very short report of an excursion into the imagination under a heading: "Why I Divorced Barbara Hutton." With a few strokes I recounted our whirlwind courtship, my proposal of marriage and acceptance by the dimestore heiress, then our honeymoon in a Maine forest retreat. The "first night," as such nights used to be called with some excitement, I told of being disturbed by a strange, crunchy-gnawing sound. In alarm at this noise, I shook Barbara but found she was already wide-eyed, that she was the cause of the sounds. She — Babs Hutton — was eating crackers in bed on her honeymoon!

Three letters from readers followed, expressing surprise that I had once been the famous person's husband, all of them wanting to hear more about Babs and Bob.

In 1958, sixty-five tourists headed by prop plane to Hawaii. They had signed up at the behest of WCCO's promotion, and I went along as the "spiritual advisor," as I laughingly called myself. The station publicity man, one Clayt Kaufman, spawned an idea about which I could generate no enthusiasm.

(Above) The dancer on the left enjoys the arrival in Honolulu of a Good Neighbor Tour in 1959. Tourists watch. He and Hurricane accompanied WCCO travelers twice to the Sandwich Islands and twice to the Far East.

(Right) WCCO's Hawaiian ice fishing stunt. The Surf Rider Hotel supplied the ice for Bob's Ice Fishing photos on Waikiki Beach, Honolulu. "The cart did not roll easily on the sand but the hotel folks cheerfully accomodated the mad Minnesotans. (Below right) Fishing through the ice. The hole is just large enough to permit an already captured mullet to peek through. Oh, publicity, publicity! Everybody knows there's no ice in the waters around the fiftieth state, but this picture made seven newspapers."

He planned a picture-taking session of me fishing through the ice of Waikiki to show Hawaiians the thrills of the St. Paul Winter Carnival in progress back in Minnesota. Decked out in swim trunks, rubber flippers, diving goggles and holding a spear, I posed on the famous sand of the famous beach to wait for the ice. Oh, yes, I also held the thick end of a bamboo pole, the business end of which had been broken off to give the pole a truncated length of about four feet. On the pole's end was tied, not a fish line, but a rope. At the rope's end, not a hook, but a fish tied through its gills. A glance should have shown anyone that this project was as phony as any piece of U.S. currency labeled "Three Dollars." Our people took snapshots; strangers looked on in amusement. From the crowd came an old duffer with a determined, snappy step, appearing not to want to miss any feature of these enchanted islands. His attire was the yachtman's type, blue coat, white cap, silk scarf at the chin — and camera. He took my picture then looked me over carefully, contemplating what he had now recorded for history. His eyes steadied on the six-inch fish dangling from the rope.

"What kind of a fish is that?" he asked.

"My friend, that is a Pacific mullet," I answered. The fish indeed was a mullet.

The old codger chomped on his false teeth and asked, "How far out did you have to go to catch that?"

"Way out . . . . . way out." Satisfied, he snapped another picture and departed up the beach in the direction of Diamond Head.

From the Royal Hawaiian kitchen came two 500-pound rectangles of ice, pushed by laughing bus boys on two kitchen carts that did not move easily over sand. In the water, I sat on one of the chunks, positioning the mullet over the hole in the ice and the photographer Kaufman had hired did the shooting.

What do I know about a publicity stunt? The picture landed on the front page of the Honolulu Advertiser and the St. Paul Pioneer Press. Kaufman is now manager of WCCO-Radio, I kid you not.

Hurricane Hat is a pretty name I invented and attached to my wife, Harriet. On the air and in correspondence, I developed this old character who became known for her belligerent tendencies, daring makeup and devotion to activism on behalf of female motorcycle riders. In competition, in debate, in interviews, in pictures, she shrilly touted the virtues of the Harley Davidson cycle and became impatient with all oppposition. My outrageous yarns about her exploits were beyond belief, or so I thought. A question regularly asked of me for years has been, "Does your wife really ride a Harley?" Most people were hesitant to be taken in, yet hesitant to be unbelieving. Some swallowed the character whole. Her marriage to the motorcycle became complete. A close golfing friend in all seriousness asked a third and mutual friend, "Does Harriet *really* ride a motorcycle?" (In truth, if by some decree all the females in the world were ordered to ride a motorcycle, my wife would be the last in the line.)

A division manager for Harley Davidson telephoned me to say that the home office in Milwaukee had received reports about my wife, and he had been asked by his superior to find out what had been going on. William H. Davidson of the motorcycle family, telephoned me on one night from a Milwaukee cocktail party where people were talking about Hurricane and her Harley. Davidson and I ever since have exchanged newsletters, his company's and my own.

The following is an annual report taken from my Christmas letter of 1973:

> *Old lovable Hurricane Hat creamed all competition at the annual Turkey Grab at Snout, Louisiana. She missed only two heads in five runs, which means she snapped off 48, a phenomenal score. She received a new award, The Golden Gamecock, for winning five years consecutively.*
>
> *South Dakotans, on Christmas Eve, heard a deep, threatening rumble, saw a blur of chrome and black, long lean forks and a fender-hugging, low profile seat. 'Twas Hurricane roaring with her holiday baskets on a preview of Harley-Davidson's big iron for 1973, the boss machine, the FX-1200.*
>
> *Stopping her long enough to get a statement for this*

sheet was difficult, but, at a gas station in Belle Fourche, she did mutter, "The big iron was made for me; I've been waiting for this for sixty years; my future now is ahead of me, unless I ride backwards." Whereupon she swung her gnarled and calloused carcass into the low profile seat and split the darkness.

(My steady readers are well aware that a Turkey Grab is a contest in which daredevils on motorbikes slalom along parallel rows of buried turkeys to grab at the heads of the fowls. Indians used to play the same game, in a milder form, on pony back. There are more intriguing details that are too gruesome for family reading.)

*   *   *

Diplomacy: the art of saying 'Nice doggie' 'til you find a rock.' — Wynn Catlin.

*   *   *

In a radio studio band rehearsal where time was fleeing, Irv Wickner, a banjo player, struck a foul note or two. The director banged his stick on the music rack bringing Wickner to his feet, expecting a reprimand. Red-faced and flustered, Wick proclaimed, "I didn't make a mistake — I just read it wrong."

*   *   *

I have belonged to four unions: The Musicians Association, The American Guild of Vaudeville Artists, the American Newspaper Guild and the American Federation of Television and Radio Artists (AFTRA). (In 1950 I was elected National Treasurer of AFTRA. You can look it up. National office was easily obtained then; you need not look that up.) I am still an active member in AFTRA.

In 1939 I worried through a strike of station employees as a member of the management faction; in three other fusses that came later, I was on the labor side. There is no comfortable position. In all businesses, as in show business, a contract yields the benefit of controlling greed on both sides.

*　　*　　*

Somewhere in the Sixties, a prominent movie personality was slated to sing at the opening of a national political convention. He was asked what number he would sing. He answered, "Oh, anything by Francis Scott Key."

*　　*　　*

Two fine quotes from the old *Collier's Weekly*:
Joe Louis, World's Champion heavyweight fighter, was sent home from a Detroit grade school with a note from his teacher: "This boy should be taught to do something with his hands."
In an article on nightclub audiences, this was printed as the wittiest putdown of a heckler by a performer: "Now look, friend, have a heart. Suppose I came over to the place where you work and knocked the pick and shovel out of your hands?"

*　　*　　*

From Public TV's show, *Good Neighbors.* — "Jerry, you are flaring your nostrils at me again."

*　　*　　*

In 1960 we landed in Tokyo and stood in line for our room keys at the Imperial Hotel. One of our group, Jim Blaul, spoke to me, "Bob, these Japanese public baths are a lot of fun a fellow back home told me. I just talked to a guy behind the desk here at the hotel about which one to go to ... he wrote out an address. Frank and I are on our way — come on along."
Frank was Frank Dobrava, a well-known Minneapolis barber and a most likable Italian. "No," came to my mind and lips,

but I didn't say a word. After an airplane ride of that length, by prop plane that stopped at Edmonton and Shemya in the Aleutians, I preferred a hotel room, my own bath and the local English newspaper. After a brief wrestle with this strong feeling, I put it down. I remember speaking to myself, "You dope, you have come a long way to see the Far East; don't hide in a hotel room and miss a Japanese bath, even if you aren't sure what that is. Live a little."

The three of us took off in a taxi with me next to the driver and my chin about three inches from the meter and my feet inside the tiny car. The happy driver stopped at a warehouse on a deserted street, which he claimed by nodding and motioning and smiling to be the place indicated by the address. We entered the building, feeling sure it was the location for the final shootout of a TV crime drama, and ascended two floors by ramp into an ordinary room. The Lady (one doesn't need language to learn who's boss) gave each of us a key and a towel and ordered, "Undress." The Lady's office and our locker room were one and the same. Jim and Frank stalled, trading guesses about what we were getting into. I shared their trepidation but charged ahead of them. In front of my locker, I stripped down to my underwear where I stopped, not knowing if this also was to be kicked off. I motioned to the Lady. She returned a gesture that said, "Of course." With my half-sized bath towel I went into the steam room at the direction of a smiling girl in white brassiere and trunks and on tiny, bare feet. In a few minutes Frank and Jim entered the steam room, talking and joking. I left them for the next attraction, the hot bath, where slabs of concrete stuck out of the walls under faucets connected to a black garden hose. An expert scrubber, female, took over.

She sponged soap on me from a bucket, sloshing water from the hose. Her deft movements were like those of a person slapping sheets on a billboard. At first, I lay face down. Her colloquial slang for our expression, "Turn the other side," was a slap on my rear. I understood. All the dust and detritus I had ferried from America on Northwest Airlines went down the drain. Jim and Frank arrived as I was finished by the slapper. Somehow in that room I lost my half bath towel.

Outside I came upon the bath itself in an enormous room that could well accomodate the swine on display at a state fair. However, the pool was small and the water very, very hot. The Japanese figures on the thermometer did not help my reporting on this matter. Near me, a large Japanese sat in a solo bath under a spout of water. He seemed a statue for the Forest Lawn Cemetery. I assumed he was a business tycoon enjoying a cleanup before going home. I was correct.

As my other two ambled poolside, I climbed out with the helping hand of a male attendant, the only male on the program. "Male masseur or female masseur?" he asked. Bravely I went, as gamblers say, for the bundle and answered insouciantly, "Female."

He ushered me to a row of twelve rubbing tables where clustered a squadron of girls in the official uniform of white pants and bras and bare feet, all chattering, flitting and flying as swallows when erupting joy in their work.

When the first of these spied me and my bulk, she released a high-pitched cry, which, translated, meant, "Look, kids, what I found." A few slaps and gestures and I flopped face down on the rubbing table, two places away from another customer, a Japanese.

In pairs, the girls worked me over by using their hands and feet. Yes, one jumped on the end of my table and started to walk up the calves of my legs, pushing and turning to produce a massaging motion. At my rib cage, this petite operator pitched onto her toes to push them between my ribs, making of herself a toe dancer and of my back a stage.

The voice of Frank and Jim came over my head. The two were being given the choice of male or female masseurs. The cowards chose male! Weaklings!

Noises of the girls' bubbling chatter never ceased and the enjoyment did not diminish. On the usual cue of a swipe on the buttock, I flipped to my back, and the toe dance from end to top started again. I wondered what the art would call for when her feet reached my abdomen. Art is the correct word. I felt her little feet arch over my stomach and onto my ribs. True, a man can become accustomed to anything — I was delighting in the dance. And Jim and Frank down the warehouse somewhere under male feet. Hah!

I shot a glance toward that near table occupied by the Japanese. The man sported a warm smile below dark and understanding eyes.

"What are you laughing at?" I asked, not expecting an answer.

"At you, my friend." This in proper American English.

"I didn't expect you to understand me," I said.

"Oh, I live in Chicago; I'm home to see my mother."

There was more for our four dollars. An exercise machine, built apparently by a committee, cold shower and then dressing at the lockers. A Japanese at a table was working on a gallon jug of beer. "Have some," he invited. I accepted. We talked. He was in construction in Honolulu, and of course, I mentioned my daughter, Helen, who was then a reporter on the Honolulu Star-Bulletin. "Look her up," I suggested.

This is what you always say to a chance acquaintance far from home, and you never expect the person to follow through. Four weeks later, my daughter wrote, "Your buddy you met in the Tokyo bath, the construction man, telephoned me, and we had a chat. Did you get clean?"

Frank and Jim arrived at the scene of the beer and lockers. We bought a gallon and shared it with the other bathers. An old Japanese custom. Comfort and companionship.

The Lady stood ready at the cash box when we prepared to leave. We deposited a wad of yen, which she carefully counted for our satisfaction and her own.

"Well," Frank announced in a display of international amity, hands across the sea and all that, "Keep the water hot."

We departed the warehouse.

*   *   *

KVOO, Tulsa, when I was on the staff in the 30's, sported a Program Director named Allan Franklin, a handsome, wavy-haired, ex-actor, the possessor of natural charm, which was embellished by stage experience and a mellifluous voice. How

Franklin loved to broadcast in front of an audience. He was hampered only by faulty eyesight in his right eye. This defect impaired his knowledge of what was going on at the Tri-State Fair. There, Allan posed with the mike at trackside, exposing his left profile and good eye to the thousands in the grandstand as he described the race cars down the track waiting for the start. Allan did not know that Art Goebel was flying at about fifteen hundred feet and about to dive in for a run before the spectators. Goebel had won the twenty-five thousand dollar first prize in a race of fliers from the West Coast to Hawaii, and he was now skywriting for Phillips 66.

The noise of Goebel's approach turned the heads of the crowd; Allan heard the same roar, but he couldn't see the plane until it levelled in front of the grandstand, puffing shots of puff to indicate he was about to start writing in the sky.

Franklin was completely surprised, but he did not fail his radio audience. He shouted over the noise, "There's some sort of delay in the race ..... and there goes Art Goebel with smoke coming out of his tail!"

The same summer, Franklin went down to Southeastern Oklahoma to report on a serious flood. On the air the guy sounded as if he were genuinely moved by the suffering and losses of the inhabitants. I sat in Tulsa listening as Allan signed off. His love of the dramatic came through.

"Ladies and gentlemen, destiny has wrought destruction today on Southeastern Oklahoma or has this been the mysterious hand of the Almighty? Certainly little men, such as I, will never know." Allan was slowing his pace obviously (to me) looking at the diminishing seconds on his watch. "The heroic work of the rescuers goes on under lantern light — water is everywhere, lapping at the destroyed homes and homeless people, but — God is in His heaven, and (another look at the watch) all I can say is .... this is KVOO in Tulsa."

We'll never know what more God or Allen would have said.

Time was up.

Along came Cedric Adams. The sweeps winner in popularity in our part of the country was one Cedric Adams. Blessed with a happy spirit and bright affection for people, he came out of a town named Magnolia, a dot on the map in the confines of the Southwestern right angle of Minnesota. As a drummer in a dance band and a summer seed salesman on the road, he put himself through, almost, the University of Minnesota. Writing a column came naturally to him, he swept up bits of information and news like a vacuum device cleans a rug. A smile and a chuckle from Cedric and a person wanted to talk and share information with this small town savant in the Big City. He made that fun. From a shopping sheet in Minneapolis he went to the dinky Minneapolis Star and to newspaper stardom later under the Cowles ownership. Radio took him on for broadcasts, and his reading audience responded loyally from the first broadcast. By personal appearances in the town and country, by writing seven days a week, by broadcasting thirteen times a week, he became a household word, to coin a phrase.

In his column he once advised housewives to beat the summer heat by standing in a bucket of water while ironing. Not good advice, but homey. And his own exclamation at the end of a bit of grisly news — "My, my!" Exact pronunciation never bothered him; he crashed into foreign place names and proper names and finished them off smoothly, not necessarily correctly. "Never stop, once you get started into a long proper name," Cedric advised.

On two occasions I remember, and there were probably more, I went into the country on my own personal appearance engagement to be greeted, "Hello, Bob. Where's Cedric?" And I was the attraction.

Cedric's listeners and readers cherished him for his small town attitudes as well as for his willingness to risk the risque and for his invariable friendliness. I have seen timid and unimportant people, families and those alone, wait for him in the station lobby. Emerging from a studio, he greeted these fans, shaking hands, sometimes sitting down and talking. Never did I see him pass up a fan or brush off one who took extra time. To him, this habit was not a practical matter that enhanced his career; you just don't dodge people who want to talk to you; that is not polite — not in Magnolia, Minnesota.

Cedric's steep level of popularity on the air and in the newspaper qualified him as a valuable prize for marauding stations and sponsors.

Rube Couch, then Sales Manager of Butternut Coffee in Omaha, went after this prize. Couch and I were friends because of the sponsorships of my morning news on the air.

The rival KSTP, owned by aggressive Stan Hubbard, the elder, joined with Couch to develop a regional network, with KSTP as the flagship, and hire Cedric away from WCCO. The plot almost worked. One scene in the drama, described by Couch, who was there, reveals Cedric clearly and charmingly. Final planning was under way in Hubbard's office. Adams, their star, was present. He was to benefit by a stiff hike in his fees for jumping with his newscasts to these different outlets. The negotiation went on and on. They reached the subject of the money figure for Cedric. Someone said, "Well, Adams, what do you think?" All eyes turned to him who had sprawled on a davenport. Cedric had dozed off to sleep.

He and I were driving somewhere together and talking shop, of course, when I asked him when he intended to retire.

"Gee, I don't know. I can't figure out how much money I need to have before I retire."

Cedric never established that retirement figure; he didn't need to. He died in 1961.

Chapter Fourteen

I'm not so young that I fight policemen just because spring
is here.

—*Don Marquis*

YOU HAVE READ to the edge of the end of my anecdotage, to this
last chapter, to the moment when the reader deserves a few
lofty and philosophical conclusions. I dont' seem to have any.

In school I was told that communication among people of
the world would achieve understanding and love. Confidently
we kids started with pen pals in Europe. Now we have instant
communication in sound and picutres through our unbeliev-
able scientific development. We find ourselves at the brink of
instant desolation through scientific development. The meek
are everywhere (and they are praying), but their inheritance of
the earth is being delayed by the political manipulators who
will live beyond their mortal years in granite in the public
square where the ultimate honor will be that which all pigeons
bestow on all statues.

Broadcasting grew up, and I went along for a living and for
the ride. The entertaining and diverting performance stabbed
the loneliness of meek people; these broadcasters sat down
with them and talked; they drew them into the affairs of the
neighborhood and state and the world and, most importantly,
the air people came back the next day (same time — same

Too Late to Classify

(Upper right) Ben Hogan, Bob Andrews of Wayzata, Minnesota and Dennis Morgan with their caddy at the Tamarisk Country Club, Palm Springs, California. 1953.

(Lower right) Russ Ewald (left) and Bob De Haven on movie set of Klang Studios in Minneapolis during the preparation of a film for the Episcopal Diocese of Minnesota. 1969.

(Below) Jack Carson thought he might be ticketed for an honorary degree at Carleton College, Northfield, Minnesota so we visited the President one Sunday afternoon. Left to right: Jack Carson and his wife, actress Lola Albright; Sid Freeman, clotheir and campus character; Laurence Gould, President of Carleton College; Bob and Harriet De Haven. P.S. No honorary degree.

(Above) Life long friends and life long tennis players. Left to right —
Neil Herman, Jack Dow, Dave Ramsay and Bob De Haven. The
latter is the author of the book, treasured by oldsters, entitled
"How To Play Tennis Without Moving." 1968.

(Upper right) The profound depths of character surface here as the
village strongman pauses from a workout to contemplate the world
and its ways. He thinks: "He quickly can I roll this barbell off my
legs and go to lunch?"

(Lower right) Our hero posing as an athlete on Minikahda Club
tennis courts in 1976. Picture is large to accomodate the showing
of the ball on left. There was no room for other players on the court.

Seventy — and still smiling!

station), ephemeral yet dependable. Broadcasters lift their listeners as one friend should life another friend. Once in a while we hold up, for a short spell, Henny Penny's falling sky. And how beautiful that the listener listens by his own choice.

A preacher once said (I was there), "Pick yourself a minor ecstasy before you petrify." A piece of news, a piece of music, a piece of a broadcaster's mind coming through the air just could be, for someone, a minor ecstacy.

In the beginning, my ecstacy was minor; in later years, the thing has become major. In the vault in the bank I have my legacy — my first fan letter. Not a letter, but a government postcard (1¢), printed with pencil, and received in November, 1930, at my Madison radio station. "Mr. Bob, you are a Class A number One radia announce."

Thanks. And shake hands with a millionaire.